"The first time we met Walt, we went to the Blue Bayou for supper—a new dining experience in itself. After pondering over what to order— we ordered steaks!!! Coming from the farmland of Southern Iowa we were steak people. Well...Walt came to our table with the biggest cleaver I've ever seen and politely said, 'If you want steaks, go down the road'—shaking the cleaver and pointing it at each of us. To say the least—we asked what HE would recommend and re-ordered. Much to our delight, the entire meal was wonderful and one we will never ever forget. Thanks, Walt!"

"Walt was fun...wine, food, laughter all made knowing him a real blessing. Working with him was always productive...what a fountain of ideas and enthusiasm. A real doer and giver of self. I will miss him..."

"Dining at the Blue Bayou when Walt walked up to my table and recognized me, I KNEW that I was somebody in the Northwoods. Once while we were waiting in the restaurant with my kids, he cooked up some frozen crawfish to show us how it was done..."

He left behind cherished memories...happy, wonderful memories... memories that will make a difference...that has already...in my life.

"He has left us...behind. But most importantly, he left behind a loving wife, three wonderful children, many friends and scores of satisfied customers.

So, Big Guy, the next bottle of Chardonnay...the next Shrimp Creole... the next Chicken Royale is for you.

We'll miss you, Big Guy.

God bless you!" .

To Rob

This is a man's

Becoming Reality!

dream.

Rita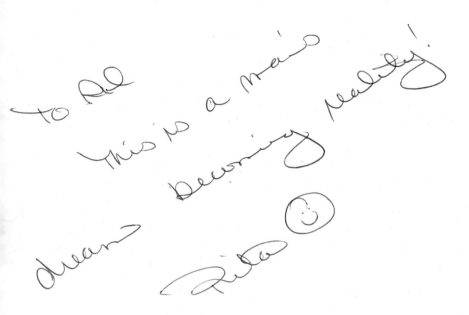

Lagniappe'
"Something a Little Extra Special"

Louisiana Cooking
from the kitchen of Chef Walter's Blue Bayou Inn

#220 of 500

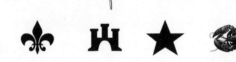

Rita M. Mazur

Walter G. Mazur

Edited by B.J. Hegeman

Illustrated by Floyd Sonnier

First Edition.

Library of Congress Catalog Card Number: 95-83544

ISBN: 0-942495-50-0 softcover book
        0-942495-51-9 hardcover book

Published by
Blue Bayou Inn
P.O. Box 115
Manitowish Waters, Wisconsin 54545

Printed by
Palmer Publications, Inc.
P.O. Box 296
Amherst, Wisconsin 54406

Dedication

To my family and friends

My goals for creating this cookbook are:

1. To acquaint you with what true Louisiana cookery is all about.

2. To take away the mystique that cooking with great taste can only be done by master chefs.

3. To explain to you where the origin of great cooking began.

4. To help you unlock your own hidden culinary talents—"the magic is in your hands."

5. Lastly—to put "fun" back into your own kitchen!

You are now asked to sit back and relax—open your heart and mind—and let Chef Walter share his years of experience with you.

Acknowledgements

...To Wayne Griffith, Woody Peterson and Don Albrecht who fanned the flames of inspiration when Walt first talked about doing his book. Walt's passing changed how we proceeded in completing the book, but we will always be grateful for their work with him in its early stages. They drafted some sample page layouts the year before Walt's death, giving him a precious sneak preview of the book he would not live to see...

...To Blue Bayou Inn Chefs Tom Mackin and Matt Metzerott, who spent hours going over the final drafts with us, helping us fill in details and figure portions that would make the recipes comprehensible for home-cooks. Their valuable input in this crucial proofing stage made the book as you see it possible...

...To David Loftus, the editor's partner and friend, who made finishing this possible. He was instrumental at several critical stages and was generous in allowing his partner time and opportunity to meet deadlines, even when it took away from their business. His unfailing support and encouragement truly paved the way to completion...

...To Thomas Koenig, a true friend, who left this world in October of 1995, but left us with these words:

> "Tend Your Own Garden
> Sow the Seed
> And Leave The Results to the Creator."

...To Floyd Sonnier, for his artwork which exemplifies his character and complements Walt's...

...To Tom Petrie, whose publishing expertise directed us to Amherst Press and Palmer Publications...

...To Ed Lump, for his eloquent words about Walt and for his formal introduction to Palmer Publications...

...And of course, to Palmer Publications and Amherst Press, especially Roberta Spanbauer and Chris Doyle. Roberta was our first contact with this outstanding company. We knew we were in trouble if we pursued it without some good, professional help. Enter Roberta, and in one short conversation we knew our prayers had been answered. Her knowledge of cookbook layout, publishing and marketing is immense and invaluable. Chris was our project manager, always available and ever-calm, even in a crisis. Her attention to detail is phenomenal and was immeasurably helpful in coaching us through the intricacies of creating clear, concise recipes for home-cooks to use and enjoy. They worked with an enthusiasm and commitment to our project that matched our own...

...To Sue Long, Boulder Junction grocer, who was generous with information that helped us to convert restaurant proportions to home-cook proportions...

...To Barb Hegeman whose commitment, determination and love of this project have made it a reality...

...Lastly, thank you to our family, friends and patrons who through the years have been the "tasters" of all these recipes.

Table of Contents

❖ 🜨 ★

On This Day...

mend a quarrel,

search out a forgotten friend.

Dismiss a suspicion,

and replace it with trust.

Write a letter to someone

who misses you.

Encourage a youth

who has lost faith.

Keep a promise.

Forget an old grudge.

Examine your gratitude.

Overcome an old fear.

Take two minutes

to appreciate

the beauty of nature.

Tell someone you love him;

tell him again,

and again,

and again.

Editor's Preface

⚜ Ⱶ ★

I've been writing all my life—newspaper articles, features, press releases, letters, you name it. Like many writers, I dreamed of writing a book someday. In the late 1980's, comparing notes with my good friend Walt Mazur, we realized he had a similar dream and eagerly agreed to combine our skills—my writing with his cooking—to make the dream come true for both of us.

Walt went to his reward in the spring of 1994. He and I had been working on the book for six years by this time, and basically, the copy was completed. You will find passages that read as though Walt is still here. These are portions of the book that were completed and passed his seal of approval. Rita, Penny and I decided to leave those parts just as he had wanted them to appear.

Each of us has added some thoughts of her own, telling you things about this friend, collaborator, husband and father that we want you to know about him. We wouldn't dare come out with such praise if he were here to red-pen it. But because he is gone, and so many reading this will never get to meet him otherwise, we are each sharing some vignettes that, combined with his comments throughout the book, allow you to enjoy his acquaintance, albeit vicariously.

This glimpse into the man behind the book is our lagniappé (something a little extra) that we think will add tremendously to your enjoyment of reading and using it. So, below are my reflections. Penny's are here as well. But be sure to turn to the back of the book, too. For once in her life Walt's wife Rita is going to get the last word. She reserved the final two pages for her comments.

I really miss my friend and mentor Walt Mazur.

When you saw this huge man lumbering out of his kitchen you were hard-pressed to predict the sprite inside him. Possessed of a mercurial mind, Walt brimmed with ideas—great, progressive expansive plans and brainstorms. And there was an incredible lightness of spirit ingrained in his very being that uplifted everyone around him. Everyone deserved a chance, respect, and dignity, in Walt's view. It is interesting that Walt titled his book Lagniappé—"something a little extra, an unexpected surprise," for that definition most aptly describes what he added to every life he touched.

Walt's advice and unfailing encouragement were the gifts he gave everyone around him every day. If you were feeling like a loser, you went to see Walt. Somehow, he could pick you up and put you back on your feet and even make you wonder how you could have thought so little of yourself, because, of course, he held you in the highest esteem.

There was another gift he gave all of us who knew him. None of us could have realized it, though, until he was gone.

You see, Walt referred to the Hereafter in very common terms, as if going to heaven was as expected and commonplace as going into Manitowish Waters for a gallon of milk. He never doubted where he'd go after his passing, and referred to his destination frequently in day to day conversation. He talked about "The Man Upstairs" as some-one with whom he had a close, personal and very friendly relationship.

This attitude was so prevalent in his speech, his thoughts, his whole presence, that a person could not think about his passing without being absolutely certain that Walt was with his Maker. Who could have guessed that every time we talked to him, Walt was comforting us. Every time I think of his passing, and start to feel badly, one of those comments comes back to me. The feeling of loss is always tempered by a vision of him serving up a "Dine With Walter" for his Friend, the "Man Upstairs."

The final gift, for me, was his insistence that his family and I see the cookbook through to publication. When someone close is dying, there is such a feeling of help-lessness. A feeling that there is nothing you can say or do for that person or for those who will be left behind.

Yet, there is nothing on earth you want more than to help in some way.

I am so grateful and proud that my friend entrusted me to assist in completing this project that was so important to him. He left me feeling like I really could do some-thing for him and for his family.

And so typical of friendship with Walt, I got more out of that final favor than any-one else. I knew Penny and Rita for as long as I knew Walt, but he was an overwhelm-ing presence, and none of us got much past being acquaintances until we were left alone with this assignment.

He did set the stage. He always spoke well of each of us to the others. And then he left us this task that brought us together and cemented the friendships he had pre-disposed. We would always have remained friends, but this project created a close-ness that was intrinsically joyful and comforting for me, and I sincerely hope for Penny and Rita as well.

His family carries on in the true spirit of lagniappé with the help of many loving friends and relatives. Walt would be so proud of the way they've pulled things together in the restaurant and continued his legacy without missing a beat. But he would not be surprised. He so consummately believed in their strength and ability that he would now comment "Of course they've carried on...of course they've done well."

When someone believes in you like that, you can do anything. Even write a book.

—B.J. Hegeman, Editor

Of all the write-ups and tributes that paid homage to Walt and the fine job he did, perhaps the one that stood out as his happiest moment professionally came when he earned a four-star rating from the tough Milwaukee Journal *restaurant critic, Dennis Getto, in a review that ran August 21, 1988. Up until that time, Blue Bayou Inn, to Walt's knowledge, was "the only restaurant north of Highway 64 to get a four-star rating from the* Journal *critic." There may have been one or two more who have scaled these heights since, but Walt was very proud to be the "first and only" for a very long time.*

WISCONSIN
THE MILWAUKEE JOURNAL MAGAZINE

August 21, 1988

Dining Out

By Dennis Getto

LOUISIANA AT ITS FINEST

BLUE BAYOU INN

Highway 51 at the Spider Lake bridge, Manitowish Waters

(715) 543-2537

★ ★ ★ ★

4 stars=excellent; 3=good; 2=average; 1=so-so; no star=poor

For years the rusty crayfish has ravaged Northern Wisconsin lakes. Now one man is turning the tables. He's chef Walter Mazur and the tables he's turning are in his Manitowish Waters restaurant, the Blue Bayou Inn.

Mazur turns the cantankerous little crustaceans into such gourmet dishes as Cajun popcorn and crawfish etouffee. Actually, only 50% of them come from the waters of Wisconsin, where they are proliferating. The rest, Mazur says, are imported from New Orleans.

Even though the chef's work with the rusty crayfish nears patriotism, you don't have to be an environmentalist to enjoy Mazur's restaurant. All you have to do is to appreciate good Louisiana-style food.

I use the term Louisiana rather than Cajun or Creole because Mazur handles both with equal aplomb. Whether it's a traditional Cajun stew like Jambalaya or a Creole gumbo soup included with dinner, the Blue Bayou's food is excellent. Before moving to Manitowish Waters, Mazur owned the Cajun House (now called Ragin' Cajun) in Chicago.

The Cajun craze has added excitement to Wisconsin dining the last few years, but it has also exacted a price. I, for one, have had it up to my necktie with token Cajun, supposedly blackened steak, fish or chicken that receives little more than a dusting of cayenne and a brief pass beneath the broiler.

Real Cajun food is a symphony of flavors that requires a maestro's hand in seasoning and preparation.

Only a few restaurants have taken Cajun cooking seriously. The Blue Bayou is one—the food I sampled as part of a dining party of six was some of the best I've eaten anywhere. (The other two outstanding places for Cajun food in Wisconsin are the Cajun Cafe above Chez Michel, 7601 W. Mineral Point Road, Madison, and the funky little Jolly Vnuk's, 2215 W. National Ave., Milwaukee.)

What made Mazur and his wife move from Chicago to the North Woods? "We came up here after Labor Day one year," he said in a telephone interview. "And we fell in love with the place."

In 1980 the couple opened the restaurant, which is about three miles southeast of Manitowish Waters. It has a pier and a patio at the rear, and the Mazurs have given a real Louisiana look to the knotty pine interior.

We realized immediately that this was not another sandwich-serving bar and boat dock. There were white cotton curtains, white tablecloths, navy blue napkins, matching stained glass, a large etched glass panel of a paddle-wheel steamboat, and waiters and waitresses in white tuxedo shirts and black ties.

The message also came through the list of New Orleans-style cocktails our waiter recited. There was a Sazerac, an old-fashioned-like drink with a dash of Pernod, named for the famous French Quarter bar in which it was invented; milk punch with bourbon, milk and sweet sugar syrup; a rum-laden Hurricane, and its smaller version, called a Squall, and a frothy gin fizz made with orange flower water and cream.

We tried one of each (preferring a squall to a hurricane) along with a soft drink and a kiddy cocktail (served at no charge) for the junior member of the group.

(In addition to its regular menu, the Blue Bayou offers either fried chicken bits or catfish tidbits at $3.95 for children 10 and under, a feature that vacationing families appreciate. The youngster in our party had the chicken, which had been done with all the care of any of the other dishes we sampled.)

A sign on the wall announced that Cajun popcorn and crawfish were available (sometimes they're not). A few minutes later, we were sharing small, shelled tails dipped in a cornmeal batter and fried pale golden. A bottle of Cajun Chef green pepper sauce accompanied them, but it wasn't overly hot. (Mazur makes and sells many of his own sauces, but nonetheless chose Cajun Chef for its mild flavor.)

Dinners included an incredibly good shrimp paté appetizer and impressive soups and salads. The paté, served with a green remoulade sauce and sprinkled with chopped black olives, was rich and creamy, with still noticeable chunks of shrimp. Its flavor was so delicate that I ate it with a fork, resisting the temptation to spread it on anything.

Cream of onion soup had been made with slowly cooked onions that imparted their wonderful sweet flavor to the cream. Seafood gumbo was dark and rich with the color and flavor of a well-made roux. It contained spicy beef sausage (which Mazur made to his own specifications), fish, rice, tomatoes, celery and homemade croutons.

Salads mixed iceberg and leaf lettuces. To serve them, our waiter wheeled over a cart laden with nine toppings: broccoli, onions, carrots, sunflower seeds, black olives, cucumber slices, green pepper slices, fresh pea pods and alfalfa sprouts, and added chosen toppings to each salad. Vinaigrette dressing was mild and well-made but I preferred the creamy Dijon with its hint of restrained mustard.

Soups and salads, served with excellent French bread, were only the opening acts for outstanding entrees.

The most unusual, alligator steaks were veal-like cutlets that had been lightly breaded, sautéed, then served in a buttery sauce. The meat's texture, denser and more tender than veal, had a rich mild flavor. Heavier spicing might have ruined it.

Crawfish etouffee, a rich dish, had been made with a lighter roux, wine, garlic, and cream and was served straight from the oven in a round casserole. Mazur departed from tradition by serving the dish with the healthier organically-grown brown rice rather than standard Louisiana white.

Brown rice also showed up in other dishes, too, such as Bayou Kitchen Jambalaya, which the menu told us had won a national rice contest prize. Shrimp, chicken, ham, tomato and pimento blended with thyme, garlic and white wine in a delightful mix of flavors.

Sweet basil shrimp took a more direct approach. A dozen medium-sized shrimp had been sautéed with garlic and a lot of fresh basil that sweetened the dish nicely.

All those restaurateurs in Wisconsin who have added token blackened entrees to their menus could learn a lesson from our meal's final entree, blackened catfish. Cookbook perfect, the fish had been coated with a mix of spices, then quickly seared in a hot skillet with a little butter. The result of such careful blackening was a spicy charcoal-like taste.

Side orders of rice fritters, hush puppies and garlic bread offered added delights. The rice fritters were soft and sweet, served hot with a dusting of powdered sugar. Hush puppies were more substantial, rich with the taste of cornmeal. And garlic bread had Parmesan cheese to perk up its flavor and paprika for eye appeal.

We were disappointed that the Bayou was out of Louisiana pecan tart, but a chocolate pecan praline tart changed our mood. A small chocolate shell had been filled with a praline-chocolate mousse, then topped with real whipped cream. Rita's cheesecake was a good icebox version of the cake made memorable by a slightly tart, brandied cranberry topping. Spumoni ice cream ran strong on pistachio flavoring and heavy on citron.

With dessert, we enjoyed the traditional coffee and chicory.

As we left the restaurant, Mazur, dressed in the traditional white coat and checked pants, thanked us for visiting. He was the one who deserved the thanks.

In Memoriam

❧ ⌘ ★

We said good-bye to Walter on Saturday, March 19, 1994. There were things in and around the service that spoke volumes about our friend.

Walter's priorities were obviously in line: Faith in God, love of family, and pride of occupation—in that order. The flowers chosen were not typical. No dour wreaths—all living, joyous plants and arrangements. Rita shared with everyone that Walt wanted it this way because he visualized death as just a step in a continuation of life. All of the songs chosen for the service were uplifting and hopeful. As an example, one was called "City of God" with the refrain "Let us build the city of God and turn our tears into dancing..." He knew where he was going.

There was an album of memories available. The family pictures reflected happy times and great love for wife and children (I remember on several Wisconsin Restaurant Association occasions seeing Walt and Rita holding hands just as sweethearts do). Most of the other pictures displayed showed pride in his restaurant and WRA. The first page contained an article about his OROY (Outstanding Restaurant of the Year award). Pictures of him and the WRA Board and miscellaneous chapter activities were prominent. He took his WRA pins and the Cajun Alligator proudly along with him.

The Homilist spoke of the man with the big presence and the even bigger heart. Walt meant something to his church and community. He was a friend and teacher they valued. Giving of himself was his trademark.

The Eulogist spoke of Walt as the "Crunch" in life. To explain this, he referred to Walt's own stated belief that to be successful in the restaurant business you had to add the "Crunch"—something that was of extra value and unexpected.

Well, Walter kept giving the "crunch" even at his funeral mass. As we recessed from the church, a staccato drum started up from behind the altar reaching a crescendo in "When the Saints Go Marching In." I think everyone lost it at that time. For just a moment I thought I had a vision of Walter following the New Orleans Jazz Band up the steps to the Heavenly Cajun Banquet awaiting him—he would order the wine.

Thanks Walt for all the "crunch" you gave us. We all will miss you....

—Ed Lump, WRA Executive Vice President, March 1994

Author's Preface

✤ 卅 ★

"Lagniappé" (lan-yap´) n. An extra or unexpected gift.

—The American Heritage Dictionary

Lagniappé, as the name connotes, is something extra—an unexpected gift—from the kitchen of Chef Walter Mazur's Blue Bayou Inn. Over the years, Manitowish Waters' visitors and residents alike have learned to eagerly anticipate the Cajun cuisine and elegant New Orleans ambiance guaranteed to greet their every visit.

Blue Bayou excellence is underwritten by a spirit of "lagniappé." Walt and his staff are dedicated to making each visit a special occasion. Unexpected gifts often appear—from unique key chains to special mints, a jar of Walt's incomparable tartar sauce or a card with an uplifting thought inscribed. Every visit is greeted by Walt's most valuable gift—his unfailing friendship and words of encouragement for every occasion. For in the Blue Bayou Inn, the words "customer" and "friend" are used interchangeably by Walter and his staff—and that's a "lagniappé" of rare and treasured quality in these frantic 1990's.

Within this "something extra special" cookbook, and true to its name, *Lagniappé* offers mouth-watering delicacies for the body, interspersed with an equally appealing and comforting set of delicacies for the soul. *Lagniappé* is something extra as much from the heart of this unique Cajun Chef as it is from his kitchen.

Like any true Louisiana Chef, Walt's heart and soul is in his cooking. In his youth he assisted his father—a skilled home chef—in working his magic on the family meals. As a young man, he chose an accounting career—but fate intervened. One of his first accounts was a hotel and Walt found himself at home in the food and beverage area of the operation.

This reunion with a childhood passion convinced him to reroute his vocation and a visit to New Orleans jelled his notions about the future. He fell in love with the authentic American cooking style he found there and worked for various New Orleans restaurants for almost six years. This experience established the foundation for his Cajun and Creole preparations.

In 1974 Walt took what he learned home to his native Chicago and opened "The Cajun House" on West Diversey Avenue. Meanwhile he married Rita, and the young couple decided that they did not want to raise their family in the city.

Seven hours north of Chicago, they found a lovely lakeside restaurant for sale on Highway 51 in Manitowish Waters, Wisconsin. They sold "The Cajun House" and in 1980 opened "The Blue Bayou Inn"—introducing the Northwoods to its first taste of Cajun and Creole cooking.

Years ahead of the Cajun craze, the Mazurs found they had some real missionary work in converting area restaurant patrons to Louisiana style gumbo, jambalaya and étouffée. When they arrived, no one else served anything like Cajun food. The area boasted great steak houses and coffee shops, with German/Bavarian inns the only real ethnic variation.

Fortunately for the Northwoods, Walt and Rita Mazur are not quitters, and the avant-garde restaurant-goers who always led the pack into any new establishment were quick to report to their friends that the food was wonderful and different and the setting was lovely. The business picked up momentum as customers learned to crave Cajun and Creole delights with the same zeal that drew them back to the area's steak houses for heavenly sirloin and T-bones and into the German restaurants for duck à la orange and wienerschnitzel.

With the national Cajun rage of the mid-1980's and a steadily growing base of loyal clientele who raved about the Blue Bayou at every opportunity, it was inevitable that the press would also "discover" it. In one year, the restaurant was written up in several publications, including the *Milwaukee Journal* and *Chicago Tribune*. Walt relates with pride that as far as he's aware, his is the first restaurant north of Wausau to earn the coveted four-star rating from the *Milwaukee Journal's* restaurant reviewer.

Last but not least, there's *Lagniappé,* a volume of recipes—and so much more. Words of encouragement for everyday life, words of encouragement for the neophyte tackling Cajun cooking for the first time.

In Walt's words, "cooking should come truly from the heart, not the mind—once you have the mechanics down.

"Don't get hung up on specific seasonings—develop a feeling, your own instinct for cooking. We all have it, but we're so hampered by society and its rules. Just think of these recipes as suggestions, things I've found worked well.

"But, when you get into your own kitchen, it's 'the magic.' I had to learn to do that. At first, I followed all the recipes to the letter—it hampered my creativity. I didn't get good at this until I learned to take Louisiana cooking as I had learned it and expand on it.

"Louisiana cooking is the only true American cooking form in the United States. It is a true outcropping of this nation as a melting pot. Cooks from a score of nationalities have contributed key elements. Although you will find the elements within the cuisine that reflect its varied heritage, Louisiana cooking on the whole is like no other on the face of the earth. The combination of the best ideas from several cuisines has been instilled with its own life and heritage by creative cooks who customized the borrowed recipes from all over the world to their environment—the fertile bayous of Louisiana.

"In the bayou they literally used the catch or game and herbs that were available at any given time of the year. True practitioners of the art of Louisiana cooking adapt to their surroundings as well. Cajun and Creole ambiance in the dish is more authentic than adherence to rigid rules and ingredients—because that's the way they really did it.

"Of course, there are some mechanics involved—a few basic spices, sauces and ingredients that lend the characteristic Louisiana flavor—but beyond that anything goes. It's your food—you don't have to go to Burger King to 'have it your way.'

"One way in which I've made a lot of adjustments is a general trend away from ingredients that we are learning will damage your health.

"Of course, when you get into any kind of cuisine, there are recipes for 'splurge' items—food that would send you to an early grave if you were foolish enough to indulge in them daily. Yet any doctor can tell you that an occasional dalliance into the world of cholesterol won't hurt you at all. Of course, the key word here is 'occasional.'

"Now when you read through this book, don't just look at the recipes you'll be fixing for family and friends. Do something nice for yourself and read the thoughts of the day. We all need a word of encouragement, especially when launching into a new project—even if it's just a new dish."

Foreword

✤ ⼐ ★

There are so many things I want to say in this foreword, I just hope it all comes out right.

First of all, I am introducing you to a wonderful collection of recipes put together by my father, Walter Mazur. He was unable to complete *Lagniappé* himself because he died of cancer on March 18, 1994. This cookbook was one of his biggest dreams, and I am proud to have the opportunity to complete it for him.

Let me tell you a little bit about my father. Our relationship was not your typical father-daughter relationship. Well, sure, if anyone could make my father mad, it was me. But I am his daughter and that is what I am supposed to do. He was not only my father, my boss and a chef extraordinaire—he was my friend. No matter what I did, my father was always there when I needed him.

My father, who was an intelligent man, did some rather comical things. When I was just seven, he decided to start my waitressing career at the Blue Bayou: cute little girl, serving lunches...well, that equals big tips. He was always thinking and adding something a little extra to all he did.

All the little extra things that he did really showed through in his "Dining With Walter." This was a special dinner at our restaurant prepared and served by my father. The dinner itself took about four hours to eat and consisted of nine courses.

This was a show he also took "on the road"—catering it in to homes if the customers wished. I remember a "Dine With Walter" that we catered at a customer's home where my father tried out a new dish. He served Shrimp Victoria over angel hair pasta. It was so wonderful that he put it onto the menu at the restaurant. My father made sure that no two "Dinings" were exactly the same, making each experience personalized and special.

My father really loved his profession and found great joy in preparing entrees that satisfied scores of customers. The pleasure he had in doing so was shown at his cooking school classes. I had the pleasure of attending quite a few of these classes. He put his heart and soul into explaining and preparing the recipes that were featured.

I consider myself lucky to have had the relationship that I did with my father. I also feel honored that people considered me his right hand at the restaurant. I remember one time when we catered a wedding—food, drinks, the whole thing. Then my father, being the character he was, decided to dance the Twist with the bride! Was I ever embarrassed! But a year later some people who had attended the wedding came into the restaurant for dinner. They told us about how everyone thought that my dad dancing with the bride was so cute, and something that they would always remember. There my father went again, adding that little extra special touch.

There are some very important people that I need to thank.

First, Mom, I want you to know how much I admire the strength and courage you have shown in the past year. I am proud to say you are my mother and I want you to know how very much I love you.

Barb, "thank you" does not seem to be big enough. Six years in the making, I know you were probably sometimes unsure if we would ever reach the end. Well, we did it, and he was laughing the whole time. Thank you for your help, guidance, pushing me to finish this, but most of all thank you for your friendship. This has been one incredible adventure and now we can celebrate.

To all of my friends, who are too numerous to mention, but especially Joel, Kim, and Missy K, thank you for all the love and support you have all given me. The late night talks, the boxes of Kleenex, and all the hugs. I would have never made it without every single one of you. Thank you so much, I love you all.

I hope that I have given you a good picture of who my father was. I have just a few more things to say.

Dad, thank you so much for being a wonderful father, teacher and friend. I know that you are smiling down on us because your dream has finally come true. I only wish that you were here with us. I miss you and love you very much.

I hope you enjoy all your cooking adventures, and remember, even great chefs like my dad sometimes burn the rice....

—Penny Mazur

If it's to be
It's up to me

Avocado Taco

I created the Avocado Taco for the special health seminars we hosted at the Blue Bayou during the early 1980's. It's a wonderful, cool summertime lunch entree when the livin' is easy...

Colby cheese in the round is by far the best for this recipe—have it sliced at the deli counter, but don't hesitate to substitute other cheeses if you cannot find Colby.

When using fresh avocados at any time, in any type of dish, always use a wooden, plastic or glass bowl. If you crush an avocado in a metal bowl, the avocado will darken.

Avocado mixture can be held for up to three days in the refrigerator.

⚜ ♓ ★

Yield: 4 servings as an appetizer, 2 as an entree

4	ripe avocados
6	green onions
1	cup sour cream
1	teaspoon chili powder
2	teaspoons cumin
	Sea salt to taste
	Cayenne or Tabasco, to taste
4	flour tortillas
4	slices Colby cheese in the round (1 ounce per slice)
1	carton (4 ounces) alfalfa sprouts

Skin, dice and mash avocados. Finely chop onions. Combine avocados, onions, sour cream, chili powder, cumin, sea salt, and cayenne or Tabasco, and mix thoroughly. Cover and chill until cold.

Place flour tortilla on a plate, cover with Colby cheese (one slice per taco). Spread alfalfa sprouts on cheese. Place a large ice cream scoop, approximately 1/2 cup, of the avocado mixture on top. Garnish with a sprinkle of paprika, cayenne and whole, pitted black olives.

~ Lagniappé ~

Blend in one additional cup sour cream and salt to taste to use as a dip for taco chips.

Deviled Eggs

✤ 戸 ★

Yield: 24 servings

12   large hard-boiled eggs
1   cup Bayou Cajun Tartar Sauce*
      Dash of cayenne
      Sea salt, to taste
      Paprika

Halve eggs. Place yolks in mixing bowl. Add Bayou Cajun Tartar Sauce, cayenne and sea salt and mix well. Spoon mixture back into egg white halves and garnish with paprika. Chill and serve.

*If Bayou Cajun Tartar Sauce is unavailable in your area, substitute Remoulade Sauce—Louisiana Style, recipe on page 103.

Vegetable Dip

*I don't have to tell people to eat their vegetables at the Blue Bayou Inn!
I just put a bowl of this dip on the table next to them, and I always get rave reviews
for the delightfully smooth blending of flavors that so perfectly complement
summer's harvest of fresh raw vegetables.*

This Vegetable Dip will hold in the refrigerator for up to a month.

Yield: 2 cups

2/3	cup sour cream
2/3	cup mayonnaise
1	tablespoon parsley flakes
1	tablespoon green onion flakes
1	teaspoon honey
1	teaspoon garlic salt
1	teaspoon Louisiana hot sauce

In a mixing bowl, combine sour cream, mayonnaise, parsley, onion, honey, garlic salt and hot sauce until smooth.

Refrigerate until well chilled. Garnish with fresh chopped parsley and a dash of paprika. Serve with fresh cut vegetables.

Marinated Shrimp

Marinated shrimp is a wonderful dish that can be served hot or cold, as an appetizer or as a delectable entree. I find that it's particularly convenient for entertaining because making it the day before and letting the flavors "marry up" overnight can actually improve the flavor! The marinade in this recipe will keep in the refrigerator up to four days, or it can be frozen in individual portions.

You'll note that there's a choice of butter or safflower oil in the marinade. I recommend butter when the shrimp will be served hot, and oil when the shrimp will be served cold.

✣ 🜨 ★

Yield: 10 to 12 servings as an appetizer, 6 to 8 as an entree

1/2	cup (1 stick) butter or 1/2 cup safflower oil	2	teaspoons dried rosemary
1/3	cup Worcestershire sauce	1/2	teaspoon celery salt
1	teaspoon sea salt	2	teaspoons olive oil*
1	teaspoon white pepper	1	tablespoon Louisiana hot sauce
2	teaspoons garlic pureé		Dash of cayenne
1	teaspoon dried thyme	3	pounds (16-20 count size) shrimp, shell on

Over low heat, melt butter or heat safflower oil in a 1 1/2-quart casserole dish. Remove dish from heat and add Worcestershire sauce, sea salt, pepper, garlic pureé, thyme, rosemary, celery salt, olive oil*, hot sauce, and cayenne.

Dehead shrimp; rinse and clean. Add shrimp to the marinade. It is best to allow the shrimp to marinate for 2 to 3 hours, or refrigerate overnight if possible, to allow all the flavors to permeate. While the dish can be cooked immediately, optimum flavor will be achieved by a longer marinating time.

When you are ready to cook the shrimp, preheat the oven to 400 degrees. Place casserole dish in oven and bake for about 12 minutes, stirring several times. Because cooking time depends on the size of the shrimp, remove a shrimp and taste. Allow the dish to cook further if necessary, up to a total of approximately 20 minutes. Do not overcook, as overcooking will make the tails hard to peel.

As an appetizer, serve hot or serve cold as finger food. Serve as an entree over natural brown rice or angel hair pasta and garnish with chopped parsley.

*If safflower oil is used, eliminate the olive oil.

Shrimp Paté

This is my own creation and is one of the many recipes included in this book "by popular demand." I've been serving it as an appetizer to my guests in the restaurant. We bring it to the table with fresh bread and our remoulade sauce (page 104), and our guests love it.

A commercial shrimp and crab boil mix may be substituted for spice bag in this recipe. Or try our own spice mix (page 78).

Yield: 10 to 12 servings

1 tablespoon mustard seed	1 1/4 pounds (30-40 count per pound) salad shrimp (thaw if frozen)
1 tablespoon fenugreek seed	
1 tablespoon thyme	3/4 pound cod, monk fish or pollack
1 tablespoon crushed bay leaves	1/2 tablespoon Louisiana hot sauce
1 tablespoon crushed red pepper	Sea salt to taste
1/4 onion	1 cup (or more) salad dressing (do not substitute mayonnaise)
1/4 lemon	
1/2 tablespoon sea salt	
1/4 teaspoon cayenne	

Place mustard seed, fenugreek seed, thyme, bay leaves and red pepper in a piece of cloth and tie it up to form a small bag. Place onion and lemon in a large pot with spice bag, salt and cayenne. Cover with water and bring to a boil over medium heat. Boil for 5 minutes. Add shrimp and fish, and cook until tender, 15 to 20 minutes. Be careful not to overcook!

Pour off water and discard spice bag, lemon and onion. Let cool. Grind shrimp and fish in a food processor or meat grinder set on fine. Add hot sauce and sea salt; mix well. Combine enough salad dressing to make a smooth, spreadable texture. Garnish with paprika and a slice of ripe olive and serve with cocktail sauce and crackers.

For hors d'oeuvres, spread paté on finger sandwiches or crackers or spoon into celery or mushroom caps. As a luncheon dish, it is marvelous stuffed in a tomato on a bed of lettuce and garnished with chopped parsley, paprika and a ripe olive.

~ Lagniappé ~

For a really special occasion, make mixture stiffer, by cutting back on the salad dressing or adding bread crumbs, and mold into a shrimp or fish. Place molded paté on a serving platter and garnish as above, using the ripe olive as the eye of your creation.

Cajun Popcorn

✤ ⊞ ★

Yield: 4 servings as an appetizer, 2 as an entree

1 **pound boiled crawfish tail meat or softshell crayfish**
2 **cups milk**
1 **cup favorite breading mix**
   Oil for deep-frying

Soak tails in milk for 5 minutes. Roll tails in your favorite breading and deep-fry for 30 to 45 seconds in oil that is kept between 335 to 350 degrees. Remove, serve with hot sauce and, of course, lots of cold beer!

Oysters Bienville

A dry or semi-dry white wine is the perfect complement to set this appetizer off!

The Bienville mixture freezes well, if you make more than you can use for one dinner. Topping mixture can be held for up to four days in the refrigerator.

Yield: 4 servings

2/3	cup plus 2 tablespoons unsalted butter	1	cup finely chopped green onions
2/3	cup whole wheat pastry flour or unbleached flour	1	cup shrimp or chicken stock
2	cups half-and-half	1/2	teaspoon paprika
1	cup milk		Dash of garlic salt
1 1/2	cups white wine		Dash of Louisiana hot sauce, or to taste
1/4	cup grated Parmesan cheese		Dash of cayenne, or to taste
1	cup fresh medium-chopped mushrooms		Sea salt, to taste
1/2	pound peeled raw shrimp, chopped fine	2	egg yolks, beaten well
		1/4	cup finely chopped parsley
			Rock salt
		1 to 2	dozen raw oysters on half shell

Over low heat, melt 2/3 cup of the butter in pan. Whisk in flour, and continue whisking over heat until mixture thickens into a light roux (see page 51). Stir in half-and-half and milk, and continue heating to thicken. Add wine and cheese and stir.

Over medium-low heat, in a separate pan, sauté mushrooms, shrimp and green onions in remaining 2 tablespoons butter until tender. Set aside.

Return roux stock to heat set at simmer and blend in paprika, garlic salt, hot sauce, cayenne, sea salt and egg yolks; let simmer for 5 minutes. Add shrimp mixture and simmer until thick, about 5 minutes. Add parsley and check seasoning. Remove from heat and allow to cool about 30 minutes, so as not to parboil oysters.

Preheat oven to 400 degrees. Spread rock salt on a baking pan. Spoon cooled sauce over oysters and place on rock salt. Bake in oven for 10 to 15 minutes, or until golden brown.

Put brown rice in 4 casserole dishes, and place oysters on the bed of rice.

Oysters Rockefeller

When the patriarch of the Antoine's Restaurant dynasty in New Orleans created this rich, elegant appetizer, he named it, appropriately, after the richest man he knew. Today, Oysters Rockefeller is still served there, made according to the original recipe created years ago by Antoine himself. The original recipe has never been given out. To this day, Antoine's is family-owned, and even staff are not privy to their secret recipe. The sauce is still prepared behind closed doors by a family member.

Spinach is usually used, but I ran across an old 1935 cookbook that called for chervil instead. While chervil is often unavailable, good fresh parsley, a close relative of chervil, is always obtainable. And it is with parsley that I prepare this delectable Oysters Rockefeller. Now, for the first time, I'm sharing this secret ingredient, along with my very own recipe for this incomparable creation.

The topping mixture can be held in the refrigerator for up to five days. It also freezes well; just roll it up and slice off the amount you would like to use.

Yield: 12 to 24 servings

6 green onions	1 cup shrimp stock
1/2 stalk celery	1/4 cup grated Parmesan cheese
1 pound fresh whole parsley	1/2 cup bread crumbs
2 cloves garlic	1 ounce Herbsainte Liqueur (a liqueur
1/2 cup butter	with an anise or licorice flavor)
1/2 cup oil	1 teaspoon salt
1 cup flour	1/4 cup white wine
1 can (2 ounces) anchovies, chopped	1-2 dozen raw oysters on the half shell
1 cup oyster water	Rock salt

Place onions, celery, parsley and garlic in a food processor or meat grinder, and grind to a very fine consistency.

In a sauté pan over medium heat, melt butter and heat oil. Whisk in flour, keeping pan on the heat and continuing to whisk until the mixture thickens to a light roux (see page 51). Stir in ground ingredients. Stir in anchovies and turn the heat down very low. Add water, stock, cheese, bread crumbs, liqueur, salt and wine. Simmer 5 to 10 minutes until heated through. Remove from heat and let mixture cool.

Spoon mixture onto oysters, or pipe onto oysters using a pastry bag.

Place rock salt on the bottom of a baking pan. Arrange oysters on bed of rock salt, and bake in 375-degree oven until edges are brown, 12 to 15 minutes.

Serve with French bread and a good Chardonnay or Pouilly Fussé.

Cajun Meatballs

⚜ Ħ ★

Yield: 12 servings as an appetizer, 4 to 6 as an entree

1	pound ground chuck
1	cup natural brown or white rice, cooked
2	teaspoons ground cumin
1	tablespoon sea salt
1/4	teaspoon cayenne
1	egg yolk
1/4	cup Bayou Cajun Mustard or German-style mustard
2	cups Bayou Cajun Barbecue Sauce*

Blend beef, rice, cumin, salt, cayenne, egg and mustard together in a mixing bowl. Shape mixture into 2-inch meatballs and place in a small baking pan. Pour barbecue sauce and 1 tablespoon water over meatballs and bake uncovered at 325 degrees for 25 minutes. Serve over rice or pasta or use as an hors d'oeuvre.

* If Bayou Cajun Barbecue Sauce is unavailable in your area, substitute Chef Walter's Barbecue Sauce, recipe on page 100.

Salads & Salad Dressings

Teach me not what you believe
But do teach me how to believe in myself

Red Bean Salad

*I call this "Trinity Salad" because of the signature trio of flavors
provided by the onions, celery and pepper.*

This salad will hold for four to five days in the refrigerator.

Yield: 6 to 8 servings

1	can (16 ounces) kidney beans
1/4	cup mayonnaise
1/4	cup chopped green onions
1/4	cup diced celery
1/4	cup diced green pepper
1/4	cup dill pickle relish
1	teaspoon Worcestershire sauce
1/8	teaspoon cayenne, or to taste, optional

In a large mixing bowl, combine beans, mayonnaise, green onions, celery, green pepper, relish, Worcestershire sauce and, if desired, cayenne for an extra kick. Mix well. Refrigerate and chill before serving.

To serve, place in your favorite serving bowl and sprinkle with freshly chopped parsley. A chopped hard-boiled egg is delicious on top of this salad as well.

Sweet & Sour Beet Salad

*I designed this recipe because beets are one of my favorite vegetables.
Remember, any recipe that is a favorite will become a signature recipe for you.
It has to taste great after you've made it so many times!*

*As with all marinated salads, it's best when left to sit overnight—
so make it the day before if you can.*

This salad will hold for up to a week in the refrigerator.

Yield: 4 to 8 servings

1   can (15 ounces) sliced beets, save half of beet juice
1   cup red wine vinegar
2   tablespoons sugar or pure maple syrup
1   tablespoon Worcestershire sauce
1   tablespoon garlic salt
    Dash of cayenne or Tabasco, optional

In a medium bowl, combine beets, reserved juice, vinegar, sugar, Worcestershire sauce and garlic salt; stir until sugar is dissolved. Add cayenne or Tabasco, if desired, for an extra spicy kick.

Chill before serving. Serve over shredded romaine lettuce.

Cucumber Salad

This is a great salad offering unusual flavors.
I consider it a wonderful addition to a buffet meal.

Cucumber Salad will hold for three to four days in the refrigerator.

Yield: 12 to 18 servings

5	medium cucumbers (8 to 10 inches each)
1	large onion
2	tablespoons sea salt
1	tablespoon celery salt
1/4	cup pure maple syrup or sugar
1	teaspoon white pepper
1	cup red wine vinegar
1	quart sour cream
1	tablespoon Worcestershire sauce
1/4	teaspoon cayenne, optional

Peel cucumbers and slice thin. Slice onion thin and halve. Mix cucumbers, onion, salt, celery salt, syrup, white pepper and vinegar into mixing bowl. Let marinate at room temperature for 1 hour. Fold in sour cream, Worcestershire sauce and cayenne, if desired, for a little extra kick. Refrigerate until well chilled. Garnish with fresh chopped parsley and green onion.

Potato Salad

I am a potato salad lover. This is an old family recipe that I particularly favor and would like to share with you. I recommend using red potatoes, as they taste just as good as the far more expensive new potatoes. I also advise that you leave the skins on the potatoes as this adds color, flavor, texture and added nutrition to the dish.

I think you'll find this a memorable accompaniment to your next picnic!

This will hold for up to a week in the refrigerator.

Yield: 12 servings

6	pounds new potatoes or red potatoes
2	medium cucumbers (8 to 10 inches each)
1	teaspoon sea salt, or salt to taste
1	teaspoon white pepper
3	tablespoons red wine vinegar
3/4	cup safflower oil or cold-pressed olive oil
1	teaspoon dill weed
1/2	teaspoon Bayou Cajun Mustard or German-style mustard

Cook potatoes until fork tender. Cool 20 to 30 minutes; then dice and place in a large mixing bowl. Peel and thinly slice cucumbers and add to potatoes. Mix in salt, white pepper, vinegar, oil, dill weed and mustard. Mix until potatoes and other ingredients are well integrated. Chill.

Serve topped with fresh chopped parsley.

Egg Salad

✤ Ħ ★

Yield: 6 servings

6   hard-boiled eggs
1/2   cup Bayou Cajun Tartar Sauce*
2   tablespoons finely diced celery
    Sea salt to taste
    Dash of cayenne, optional

Chop eggs medium and combine with tartar sauce, celery, salt and cayenne in a bowl. Chill and serve with shredded lettuce on whole wheat bread.

* If Bayou Cajun Tartar Sauce is unavailable in your area, substitute Remoulade Sauce—Louisiana Style, recipe on page 103.

Tuna Salad

✦ 🀄 ★

Yield: 3 cups

1   can (12 ounces) water packed tuna
1/4 cup finely diced celery
1/4 cup shredded carrots, optional
1   cup Bayou Cajun Tartar Sauce*
     Sea salt to taste
     Pinch of cayenne, optional

Combine tuna, celery, carrots, tartar sauce, salt and cayenne. Mix well. Chill and serve by stuffing into a tomato half or over shredded romaine lettuce. Garnish with a dash of paprika.

* If Bayou Cajun Tartar Sauce is unavailable in your area, substitute Remoulade Sauce—Louisiana Style, recipe on page 103.

Chicken Salad

Yield: 4 cups

2	cups diced cooked chicken
1/2	cup finely diced celery
1/2	cup fresh frozen peas
1	cup Bayou Cajun Tartar Sauce*
	Sea salt to taste
	Pinch of cayenne, optional

Blend chicken, celery, peas, tartar sauce, salt and cayenne until combined. Chill and serve with whole wheat toast points. Garnish with paprika.

* If Bayou Cajun Tartar Sauce is unavailable in your area, substitute Remoulade Sauce—Louisiana Style, recipe on page 103.

Caesar Salad Dressing

This recipe calls for either safflower or olive oil, but a blend of the two oils makes this dressing especially delectable.

Serve a nice Chardonnay or Fumé Blanc with Caesar Salad—it's simply outstanding! Also try the dressing over artichoke hearts; just let marinate for about an hour.

This salad dressing will hold for a month in the refrigerator.

Yield: 5 to 6 cups

1/2	bulb garlic	1	tablespoon dry mustard
1	can (2 ounces) anchovies	1	tablespoon sea salt or to taste
	Juice of 1 lemon	2/3	cup white wine (chablis preferred)
2	tablespoons Worcestershire sauce	2/3	cup red wine vinegar
1/4	cup horseradish	4	cups safflower or cold-pressed
1/4	cup grated Parmesan cheese		extra virgin olive oil
1	egg, coddled		

Mince garlic cloves and anchovies into a paste. Add the following one at a time, mixing after each addition: lemon juice, Worcestershire sauce, horseradish, cheese, egg, mustard, salt, wine and vinegar.

Let sit for about 15 minutes. Add oil in a slow steady stream, whisking until fully incorporated. Store in a tightly sealed container.

For salad—by Caesar...

Wash and cut romaine lettuce into bite-sized pieces, preparing about 1 cup per person; that's usually enough for salad size. Pat or shake dry. Keep refrigerated until needed. Any salad tastes better when the greens are nice and cold. Mix romaine lettuce with 1 ounce dressing per serving in a bowl, then dish out individual servings. Place a few croutons on the salad and sprinkle with fresh grated Parmesan cheese.

~ Lagniappe~

Romaine lettuce is listed high on the nutrition list because it is better by far than any other green given to us by the GOOD MAN. Spinach runs a close second. I like combining fresh romaine and spinach as a base for Caesar Salad or any salad for that matter!

Grecian Salad Dressing

This dressing is great on an all-green salad, or on a layered salad of sliced tomato, white or red onion and cucumber. Drizzle dressing on the salad about an hour before dinner and let the dressing marinate the veggies—outstanding!
Garnish with fresh, chopped parsley.

When preparing the dressing, be sure to rub the oregano leaves between your hands over the mixing bowl to release the herb's oil and flavor.

This dressing will hold indefinitely in the refrigerator.

Yield: 4 cups

1	can (2 ounces) anchovies, optional
1	cup red wine vinegar
2	teaspoons sea salt*
1/2	teaspoon white pepper
1	teaspoon sugar or pure maple syrup
3	teaspoons dry mustard
3	teaspoons dried oregano leaves
2	cloves garlic, minced
2	teaspoons lemon juice
3	cups extra virgin olive oil or safflower oil

Mash anchovies in a medium bowl. Add vinegar, salt, pepper, sugar, mustard, oregano, garlic and lemon juice, and mix to combine.

Let sit for 20 minutes. Slowly add oil in a thin stream, stirring constantly.

Store dressing in a tightly sealed container in the refrigerator.

*If anchovies are used, then use sea salt to taste.

Hazel Dressing

This is an old recipe I found years ago. I adapted it to my liking, and I've been using it ever since. I'm not sure how it got the name, but I suspect it originated with a lady named Hazel.

This dressing will hold for up to a month in the refrigerator.

Yield: 1 1/2 cups

1/2	cup safflower oil
1	cup chopped green pepper
1/2	cup tomato sauce
1	tablespoon red wine vinegar
2	teaspoons sugar or pure maple syrup
1	teaspoon white pepper
1	teaspoon minced garlic
1	teaspoon Tabasco, or to taste
1/4	teaspoon cayenne
1/2	teaspoon sea salt

Mix oil, green pepper, tomato sauce, vinegar, sugar, white pepper, garlic, Tabasco, cayenne and salt by hand or in a blender until all ingredients are blended and smooth.

Store in a tightly sealed container in the refrigerator. To bring out the full flavor of the ingredients, remove just enough dressing for the meal a half an hour before serving and let warm to room temperature.

Honey Roquefort Dressing

Let's lay this one to rest once and for all.
Are blue cheese and Roquefort cheese one and the same?

NO!

Yes, they are similar in taste and texture. However blue cheese is made from cow's milk and injected with mold enzymes. True Roquefort cheese is made from ewe's milk, injected with moldy bread crumbs (really!) and ripened in caves. My son Joe and I love both cheeses, and that's why you'll find more than one recipe using these beloved cheeses.

Yield: 4¹/₂ cups

2	cups safflower or olive oil
1	cup honey
1/2	cup red or white wine vinegar
2	egg yolks, fully cooked and mashed
1/2	pound Roquefort or blue cheese

In a mixing bowl, blend oil, honey, vinegar and egg yolks. Crumble cheese and gently stir into the mixture.

Roquefort/Blue Cheese Dressing

*Roquefort or blue cheese is wonderful in or with this creamy salad dressing,
but don't overmix. Adding cheese with all the other ingredients in the blender
or mixer will break it up and destroy the wonderful texture and bursts of flavor
achieved by leaving it lumpy. Try adding the cheese sprinkled over the salad
as you serve it, instead of mixing it in; it's in your "magic hands."*

Yield: 2 1/2 cups

1 1/2	cups safflower oil or cold-pressed olive oil
1/2	cup red wine vinegar
1 1/2	teaspoons sea salt
	Dash of cayenne
1/4	teaspoon paprika
1 1/2	teaspoons sugar
1/2	cup crumbled or chopped Roquefort or blue cheese

Combine oil, vinegar, salt, cayenne, paprika and sugar, and mix or blend until smooth. Gently stir in cheese.

Buttermilk Roquefort/Blue Cheese Dressing

I particularly like this one served over chopped fresh spinach!

Yield: 6 cups

1/2	cup buttermilk
2	cups sour cream
3	cups mayonnaise
1/2	teaspoon chicken base
1	tablespoon lemon juice
1	teaspoon garlic salt
1/2	teaspoon salt
	Healthy dash of Louisiana hot sauce
1/2	pound blue or Roquefort cheese

Blend buttermilk, sour cream and mayonnaise until smooth. In a separate bowl, dissolve chicken base in a small amount of water. Add dissolved chicken base, lemon juice, garlic salt, salt and hot sauce to mayonnaise mixture. Once again blend until smooth. Crumble cheese and very gently mix into dressing. Chill and serve.

Sour Cream Dressing

*I think this is a wonderful dip for appetizers, vegetables, chips or fresh fruit.
Omit the hot sauce and cayenne if dressing/dip is to be used on fruit;
or give it a try—you MAY like it!*

Lite cream cheese or yogurt may be substituted for sour cream.

This dressing will hold in the refrigerator for up to a month.

Yield: 1 1/2 cups

1	cup sour cream
1	tablespoon lemon juice
1	tablespoon horseradish
2	tablespoons sugar or pure maple syrup
1/4	teaspoon sea salt, or to taste
1/2	teaspoon dry mustard
	Dash of hot Louisiana sauce
	Dash of cayenne

Whip sour cream until fluffy. Fold lemon juice, horseradish, sugar, salt, mustard, hot sauce and cayenne into sour cream. Chill before serving. Garnish with chopped parsley if you wish to use it as a dip.

Cottage Cheese Salad Dressing

*This is an old recipe I've had for years, and it's still a favorite.
And so simple. Try it, you'll like it!*

This recipe will hold for up to a month in the refrigerator.

Yield: 1 1/2 cups

3/4	cup sweetened condensed milk
1/2	cup creamed cottage cheese
6	tablespoons red wine vinegar
1/2	teaspoon sea salt
3/4	teaspoon dry mustard
1/2	teaspoon paprika

Combine milk and cottage cheese. Blend in vinegar, salt, mustard and paprika. Beat with rotary egg beater until mixture is smooth, well-blended and thick. Pour into a tightly sealed container and chill to "marry up" all the flavors.

To bring out the full flavor of the ingredients, remove just enough dressing for the meal a half an hour before serving and let warm to room temperature.

Thousand Island Dressing

This is a great recipe—don't let the simplicity fool you!

This dressing will hold for about a month in the refrigerator.

Yield: 2 cups

1	hard-boiled egg
2	tablespoons dill pickle relish
2	tablespoons finely chopped white onion
1/4	cup chili sauce
2	tablespoons tomato paste
1	teaspoon Worcestershire sauce
1 1/4	cups mayonnaise
1/4	teaspoon Louisiana hot sauce

Chop hard-boiled egg. Combine egg, relish, onion, chili sauce, tomato paste, Worcestershire sauce, mayonnaise and hot sauce in a mixing bowl until well-blended. Refrigerate and serve chilled.

Cajun House Dressing

*I created this recipe for my first restaurant,
the Cajun House on West Diversey Avenue in Chicago.*

Yield: 8 cups

1	quart salad dressing or mayonnaise
1/2	cup Bayou Cajun Mustard or German-style mustard
6	tablespoons Worcestershire sauce
1 1/2	cups white wine
1	tablespoon sweet basil
1	tablespoon gumbo filé powder
1	tablespoon thyme

Place dressing, mustard, Worcestershire sauce, wine, basil, filé powder and thyme in a mixing bowl. Blend thoroughly. Pour into a tightly sealed container and refrigerate.

To bring out the full flavor of the ingredients, remove just enough dressing for the meal a half an hour before serving and let warm to room temperature.

Cucumber Dressing

I ran across this recipe many years ago and find it to be exciting and refreshing as well as something a little unusual. When you find yourself looking for something a little different than "hitting the bottle" of commercial salad dressing in the fridge, bring yourself out of the doldrums with this tasty alternative.

This dressing will hold for up to a month in the refrigerator.

Yield: 6 cups

3	large cucumbers, peeled
1	bunch fresh dill
5 to 6	green onions
12	sprigs parsley
1	tablespoon sea salt, or to taste
1/2	cup red wine vinegar
1/2	cup Bayou Cajun Mustard or German-style mustard
1	cup white wine
1	teaspoon black pepper
1	tablespoon Tabasco
2	tablespoons celery seed
1	quart sour cream

In a food processor or meat grinder, grind cucumbers, dill, onions and parsley together in a coarse grind. Add salt, vinegar, mustard, wine, pepper, Tabasco, celery seed and sour cream. Blend together.

Refrigerate a few hours to chill and "marry up" the flavors. To bring out the full flavor of the ingredients, remove just enough dressing for the meal a half an hour before serving and let warm to room temperature.

Peanut Dressing

*This is a wonderful dressing not too many people know anything about—
that's because I created it myself. I found a recipe for peanut soup,
and that gave me the idea to try a peanut dressing.
You just won't believe it!*

This dressing will hold for up to a month in the refrigerator.

Yield: 10 cups

1/3	cup peanut butter
1/4	cup horseradish
2	quarts salad dressing or mayonnaise

Place peanut butter, horseradish, 1 cup water and salad dressing in a blender or mixing bowl. Mix until well-blended. Serve chilled over your favorite green salad.

Caraway Seed Dressing

*I am a lover of great salads and enjoy creating unusual salad dressings
using some of the terrific herbs often overlooked in dressing preparation.
Give this a try—you may end up hooked on it just like I am.*

Caraway Seed Dressing will hold for up to a month in the refrigerator.

Yield: 6 cups

1/2	tablespoon sea salt
1/4	cup white wine
1/4	cup red wine vinegar
2	tablespoons Bayou Cajun Mustard or German-style mustard
1	quart salad dressing or mayonnaise
1	tablespoon caraway seed
1/2	cup horseradish

Thoroughly mix salt, wine, vinegar, mustard, salad dressing, caraway seed and
horseradish in a mixing bowl.

Pour into a tightly sealed container, and store in refrigerator until ready to use. To
bring out the full flavor of the ingredients, remove just enough dressing for the meal a
half an hour before serving and let warm to room temperature.

Celery Seed Dressing

This dressing will hold for up to a month in the refrigerator.

Yield: 10 cups

1/2	cup sugar or pure maple syrup
2	tablespoons dry mustard
1	cup white wine (chablis preferred)
2	quarts salad dressing
1/4	cup celery seed

Place sugar, dry mustard and wine into mixing bowl. Mix thoroughly. Add salad dressing and celery seed; mix well.

Store in a tightly sealed container. Refrigerate until ready to use. To bring out the full flavor of the ingredients, remove just enough dressing for the meal a half an hour before serving and let warm to room temperature.

Mustard Seed Dressing

I recommend that this salad dressing be made up ahead using all the ingredients except the Miracle Whip, because the completed mixture is best when held only a day or two, while the concentrate minus the Miracle Whip can be held for months under refrigeration. Then when you're ready to use it, blend one part concentrate to five parts Miracle Whip to make whatever amount you wish.

✦ Ⱨ ★

Yield: 10 cups dressing or 2 cups concentrate

1/4	cup dry mustard
1	tablespoon lemon juice
1/4	cup fresh chopped parsley
2	tablespoons Worcestershire sauce
1/2	cup Bayou Cajun Mustard or Dijon mustard
2	tablespoons whole mustard seeds
1/2	cup dry white wine
2	quarts Miracle Whip salad dressing

Combine dry mustard, lemon juice, parsley, Worcestershire sauce, mustard, mustard seeds and wine in a bowl. Mix thoroughly. Let mixture "rest" for 15 to 20 minutes to combine flavors. At this point, mixture may be stored in a tightly sealed container and refrigerated.

When ready to use, whip in 5 parts Miracle Whip to 1 part concentrate for amount of dressing you need (or 3 teaspoons concentrate to 1/4 cup Miracle Whip per serving).

~ Lagniappé ~

Substitute sour cream for Miracle Whip to make a wonderful dip.

Creole Vinaigrette Dressing

✦ Ⱨ ★

Yield: 3¹/₂ cups

1/2	cup red wine vinegar
1/2	tablespoon paprika
1/2	cup Bayou Cajun Mustard or German-style mustard
1/2	tablespoon salt
1/8	teaspoon cayenne
1/4	cup white wine
1/2	tablespoon hot sauce
	Juice of 1/4 lemon
2	cups salad oil

Combine vinegar, paprika, mustard, salt, cayenne, wine, hot sauce and lemon juice in a mixing bowl or a blender. Mix until smooth. Whisk in oil in a slow steady stream, or blend at low speed, until incorporated. Store in a tightly sealed container. Refrigerate until ready to use.

To bring out the full flavor of the ingredients, remove just enough dressing for the meal a half an hour before serving and let warm to room temperature. Serve over cooked shrimp or green salad.

Vinegar Salad Dressing

✤ Ⱨ ★

Yield: 3 1/2 cups

2 1/4	cups safflower or cold-pressed olive oil
3/4	cup red wine vinegar
2	tablespoons Bayou Cajun Mustard or German-style mustard
1/2	teaspoon salt
1/8	teaspoon white pepper
1/2	teaspoon garlic powder
1/2	tablespoon sugar

Combine oil, vinegar, mustard, salt, pepper, garlic powder, sugar and 6 table-spoons water; mix well. Before serving, let sit at room temperature for 2 hours to allow flavors to "marry up."

Store in a tightly sealed container. Refrigerate until ready to use. To bring out the full flavor of the ingredients, remove just enough dressing for the meal a half an hour before serving and let warm to room temperature.

T & M Dressing

✤ Ħ ★

Yield: 7 cups

1	can (46 ounces) tomato juice
1/2	pound Swiss cheese, grated
1/4	cup Bayou Cajun Mustard or German-style mustard
	Dash of sea salt, or to taste
	Dash of cayenne, or to taste

Place tomato juice, cheese, mustard, salt and cayenne into blender, and mix until smooth. Refrigerate.

Soups, Gumbos, Rice & Vegetables

FLOYD SONNIER
LOVE ON THE BAYOU © 5/94

*Find the sunshine within your heart
and all your days will be bright!*

Soup Stock

Soup Stock is easy to make and basically consists of using shells or bones that are infused with wonderful flavors to enhance your soups and other stock-based recipes. Stock will keep overnight in the refrigerator and for several months in the freezer if it is stored in a tightly sealed container.

Shellfish Stock

Yield: 3 cups stock

1   pound shells of shrimp, crayfish or lobster
1   quart water
1/2   tablespoon sea salt

Simmer shells, water and salt until volume is reduced by one-third, 20 to 30 minutes. Remove shells and use in desired recipe.

Poultry & Meat Stocks

Yield: 1 quart stock

2   pounds bones from type of meat desired
6   cups water
1/2   tablespoon salt

Simmer bones, water and salt in a large stock pot for 4 to 6 hours. Remove bones and use in desired recipe.

Roux

⚜ ⪥ ★

A roux is a mixture of equal parts flour and fat used to thicken soups and liquids. It is the basis of many hearty Louisiana recipes such as gumbos, étouffées, bisques and stews.

There are three absolutes about making roux. First, it is always one part flour to one part oil (or butter or other type of fat). Second, you start by heating the oil in the pan, adding the flour a little at a time. Third, whatever you do, NEVER stop stirring or whipping the mixture while that pan is hot (cooking doesn't stop when you turn the heat off—it stops when the pan cools).

Individual recipes will call for the type of fat to be used in the roux and the color the roux should be (light, medium or dark). These two factors will affect the amount of time it takes to make the roux.

If the recipe calls for whole butter, you may spend 45 minutes making your roux since you must always use very low heat. Using clarified butter (whey removed) or other oils, the roux can be cooked over medium heat and the time to make it will be shorter.

Over medium heat, using an oil, it will take you only 2 to 3 minutes to make a light roux (barely colored or chalky), 5 to 7 minutes to make a medium roux (golden straw-colored with a slightly nutty aroma) and 7 to 8 minutes to make a dark roux (milk chocolate colored, with a pronounced nutty aroma).

Don't be discouraged if you burn the roux your first few attempts. If you have never made roux before, be prepared with extra flour and oil to give it a few attempts. If the first batch burns, lower the temperature and try again. If you lower the temperature, you will need more time to bring it to the desired color—but you will also have more time to react to changes in consistency and color.

With a little experimentation you will develop the method you are most comfortable with. And once you find the method that comes most easily to you, continue to use it so that roux-making becomes second nature to you.

One final tip about roux-making. Have the ingredients for the next step in your recipe ready to add the moment the roux reaches the desired color. The addition of these ingredients will stop the action and hold your roux at the desired point of doneness.

French Onion Soup

French onion is a classic soup, but this version has some of my own personal touches. One of these is dry vermouth; it is made from herbs and spices and adds a wonderful touch to the flavor. I think you'll find this soup terrific.

In the recipe below, substitute three quarts beef stock for beef base and water if you wish.

French Onion Soup can be held in the refrigerator for up to four days.

Yield: 12 bowls or 20 cups

1/4	cup plus 2 tablespoons unsalted butter or vegetable oil, divided
1/4	cup whole wheat flour
1 1/2	pounds white onions, sliced thin and quartered
1 to 3	teaspoons sugar, optional
2	cloves garlic, minced
1/4	cup soy sauce
1/4	cup beef base
3	quarts water
	Dash of Louisiana hot sauce
	Sea salt to taste
1 1/2	cups dry vermouth

Heat 1/4 cup of the butter or oil in a saucepan. While continuing to heat, slowly whisk in flour to make a light roux (see page 51).

In a separate pan, over medium-low heat, sauté onions in remaining butter or oil until golden brown, about 25 minutes. If desired, add sugar, a little at a time up to 3 teaspoons, to help the browning process. Add garlic about 5 minutes before removing onions from the pan.

Place soy sauce, beef base, water, hot sauce, salt and dry vermouth into a soup pot. Bring to a boil over medium heat, then add sautéed onion. Add roux and continue cooking until entire mixture is thoroughly heated, 5 to 10 minutes. Stir while heating, as roux may cause mixture to stick.

Serve soup in a cup or bowl, and top with croutons or Parmesan cheese.

~ *Lagniappe* ~

Pour hot soup in ovenproof bowls or cups and top with Swiss cheese, then brown in the oven for a wonderfully unique and appealing presentation.

Creole French Onion Soup

You'll get rave reviews from all with my version of this delightful soup.

In the recipe below, three quarts chicken stock may be substituted for chicken base and water.

Creole French Onion Soup can be held in the refrigerator for up to five days.

Yield: 8 bowls or 12 cups

1/4	cup chicken base
3	quarts water
1	tablespoon Worcestershire sauce
1	tablespoon Louisiana hot sauce
1	pound white onions
1/4	cup unsalted butter
1	cup vegetable oil
1	cup whole wheat flour
	Dash of cayenne
	Sea salt to taste

Place chicken base, water, Worcestershire sauce and hot sauce in a soup or stock pot. Simmer for 25 to 30 minutes.

Meanwhile, cut onions into medium slices. Melt butter in a sauté pan over low heat until slightly browned. Add onions and cook until golden brown, about 25 minutes. Add cooked onions to stock pot, continuing to simmer.

Heat oil in a saucepan and slowly whisk in flour to make a light roux (see page 51).

Add roux to stock pot, stirring continuously with a whip to prevent burning. Add cayenne and salt and heat soup almost to the boiling point, then whip thoroughly. Reduce heat and simmer for 5 to 10 minutes.

Serve in a cup or bowl. Top with homemade croutons and Parmesan cheese.

Peanut Soup

*I was looking for something different in a soup and came up with this one.
I love peanuts, so when I found a soup recipe that used them, I worked on it until
I came up with a flavor I was happy with—and that is what I serve today.*

In the recipe below, chicken stock may be substituted for water and chicken base.

This soup will hold in the refrigerator for four to five days.

Yield: 12 bowls or 16 cups

2	quarts water
2	tablespoons chicken base
1	quart milk
1 1/2	cups peanut butter
1	teaspoon Louisiana hot sauce
1	cup vegetable oil
1	cup whole wheat flour

In a soup or stock pot, heat water, chicken base, milk, peanut butter and hot sauce over low heat.

In a saucepan, heat oil and slowly whisk in flour to make a light roux.

Raise heat under stock pot to medium and add roux, stirring with a whip until mixture is well-blended. Continue to heat until mixture reaches the boiling point, stirring often to prevent roux from sticking. Reduce heat to low and simmer until the soup thickens, about 5 minutes.

Serve in a cup or bowl, garnished with chopped peanuts and chopped parsley.

~ Lagniappé ~

For a REAL twist, add grape jelly before serving. *

*Editor's Note: "April Fool." Walt gave me this information when we worked on the recipe and I never had a clue it was a joke until Matt & Rita were looking over recipes in the initial proofing stage and they started laughing. They say Walt was joking— never ever saw him do this.... He'd love it—knowing he "got" me even a year and a half after he was gone. He even let it pass in his proofing!

Bayou Country Chili

As with all great soups, gumbos and chilies, this tastes best the next day.
So make it a day ahead!

You can refrigerate this chili for up to a week or freeze it for up to six months.

Yield: 10 bowls or 16 cups

2	cups dried red beans	2	cans (one 16 ounces and one 8 ounces) diced canned tomatoes or 1 1/2 pounds fresh tomatoes, diced
1/2	cup vegetable oil		
1/2	cup whole wheat flour		
2	green peppers, medium chopped		
3	cups medium chopped white onion	1/2	cup chili powder
1/2	cup medium chopped celery	2	tablespoons ground cumin
1/4	cup chopped fresh parsley	2	tablespoons beef base
2	cloves garlic, finely chopped	1/2	tablespoon sea salt, or to taste
1	pound ground lean beef or turkey	1/2	tablespoon crushed red pepper
3/4	pound all beef smoked sausage, ground	1	tablespoon dried thyme
		1/2	teaspoon white pepper
		1/2	teaspoon cayenne, or to taste

Place beans in a large pot with water equal to 3 times the volume of beans. Soak beans at room temperature overnight or for at least 3 to 4 hours. Rinse off and add fresh water. Place pot over high heat until water boils. Shut off heat, cover and let sit on burner for 10 minutes.

Turn heat to low and simmer for an additional 30 to 45 minutes, or until beans reach the desired tenderness. When beans are tender, cover and remove from heat and let "rest" for 30 minutes.

Pureé 1/3 of the cooked beans with all of the liquid in blender to bring out more flavor and to provide a thickening agent for the chili. Return to pot with beans.

In a large sauté pan, heat oil and slowly whisk in flour to make a roux (see page 51). Continue heating and whisking until roux turns dark brown. Add green peppers, onion, celery, parsley and garlic to roux and sauté over medium heat until tender and onions are translucent, about 20 minutes. In a separate sauté pan, brown beef and sausage over medium heat.

Combine beans, ground beef, sausage, tomatoes, chili powder, cumin, beef base, salt, red pepper, thyme, white pepper and cayenne in large stock pot and bring to a boil.

Reduce heat and simmer for 30 minutes. Add roux mixture and simmer on low heat for 15 minutes. Stir often as the roux may cause the chili to stick. Check for taste of seasoning.

Serve with brown rice and chopped green onion for garnish. French bread is a must! How 'bout one big glass of beer! YES!!

Bayou Creole Turtle Soup

I spent two years developing this recipe, working to bring out what I thought Louisiana turtle soup should be. I consider this to be one of my finest recipes.

It's also one of those wonderful recipes that takes some time and effort to make, but you will be rewarded by its fantastic taste! So make plenty to freeze, and it'll be ready when you get a craving for this rich Louisiana flavor.

Bayou Creole Turtle Soup will hold for up to four days in the refrigerator or for months frozen in individual portions. And like so many wonderful soups and stews, reheating only makes it better than it started out....

Baby alligator meat can be substituted for turtle following the same cooking method.

By the way, a good merlot becomes great when sipped while eating my turtle soup!

Yield: 16 bowls or 26 cups

2¹/2	pounds turtle meat with bone in	1/2	cup Worcestershire sauce

2½   pounds turtle meat with bone in
1   tablespoon sea salt
1   large onion
1/2   clove garlic, finely chopped
1/2   stalk celery
12   sprigs parsley
1   cup oil
1   cup whole wheat flour
3   cans (16 ounces each) crushed
         tomatoes

1/2   cup Worcestershire sauce
1/4   teaspoon ground allspice
1/4   cup beef base
1/4   teaspoon cayenne
1/2   teaspoon crushed red pepper
1/2   teaspoon black pepper
1 1/2 tablespoons dried thyme
2   bay leaves
1 3/4 cups dry sherry or vermouth

Place turtle meat in stock pot with 2 quarts water and salt. Bring to a boil on high, then turn down to simmer, cooking until meat falls from the bones, 3 to 3½ hours. Remove meat from the pot, reserving pot and turtle stock.

Remove meat from bones; discard bones and allow meat to cool, about 30 minutes. In a food processor or meat grinder, grind the meat and set aside.

Grind onions, garlic, celery and parsley and set aside.

Heat oil in a medium pot, and make a roux by adding flour, whisking continually (see page 51). When the roux has achieved a rich dark color, add the ground vegetables and parsley. Stir to combine and simmer about 20 minutes, until celery is tender and onions are translucent.

In the stock pot containing the turtle stock, add tomatoes, Worcestershire sauce, allspice, beef base, cayenne, crushed red pepper, black pepper, thyme, bay leaves and roux mixture. Stir mixture to combine and continue to stir occasionally to prevent roux from sticking. Bring the entire mixture up to a boil, then turn down to simmer until the mixture is heated thoroughly, 5 to 10 minutes.

Add the turtle meat and simmer another 5 to 10 minutes, until the turtle meat has been brought up to the temperature of the rest of the mixture. This allows the flavor of the turtle to blend with the rest of the soup without breaking down. It is important not to add the meat too early in the cooking process, or it will stick to the bottom of the pot and ruin the flavor of the soup. Stir in sherry just before removing the soup from the heat. Remove bay leaves before serving.

Garnish soup with a generous amount of finely chopped green onion. Serve with a dish of rice on the side.

Upon request, turtle soup can also be served with chopped hard-boiled egg on the side or on top. Add some French bread and you have a meal!

~ Lagniappé ~

Turtle soup is generally served with the sherry on the side.
I recommend adding it at the end of the cooking process to allow the flavor to cook through the soup. This also allows the amount to be controlled so there is neither too much or too little.

Shrimp & Okra Gumbo

Traditionally, a great gumbo is made with a roux. The okra in this recipe makes the roux unnecessary because of the vegetable's natural thickening characteristics. This is one of the thickest soups you'll eat, yet it's thickened only by the wholesome delicious okra itself! This gumbo is one of my favorites!

Never use a cast iron pot for cooking okra, as it will cause the okra to turn black.

Shrimp & Okra Gumbo freezes well, or it will hold in the refrigerator for up to five days.

Yield: 12 cups

1/4	cup Louisiana hot sauce
1	teaspoon plus 1 tablespoon sea salt, divided
2	pounds (31 to 35 count) peeled shrimp, shells reserved
2	cups diced onions
1/3	cup unsalted butter
1	green pepper, diced
3	pounds fresh okra, chopped, or frozen, thawed
2	cups crushed tomatoes,
	or 3 fresh tomatoes, peeled and chopped
1	clove garlic, chopped
2	tablespoons chopped fresh parsley
	Dash of salt, or to taste
	Dash of cayenne, or to taste
	Dash of Louisiana hot sauce, or to taste

Combine hot sauce and 1 teaspoon of the salt. Cover shrimp with mixture and let marinate for 20 minutes or more at room temperature.

Place shrimp shells in a pot with 2 quarts water and remaining 1 tablespoon salt. Simmer until water is reduced by one-third, 20 to 30 minutes. Strain shrimp stock, and discard shells.

Over medium-low heat, sauté onions in butter until golden brown, about 25 minutes. Add green pepper and okra, and continue to sauté until just tender, about 10 minutes. Add shrimp, tomatoes, garlic, parsley, salt, cayenne, hot sauce and 2 1/2 cups shrimp stock. Simmer 15 to 20 minutes. More shrimp stock may be added if mixture needs moisture. Too much shrimp stock will make the dish too salty, so add more sparingly and check the flavor of the dish as you do. Reserve remaining shrimp stock for other recipes.

Serve with natural brown rice and hot French bread.

Chicken & Okra Gumbo

This gumbo can be refrigerated for up to five days or frozen up to six months.

Yield: 12 bowls or 20 cups

1 large chicken (3 to 5 pounds)
1/4 cup hot sauce
1 teaspoon salt
4 tablespoons safflower oil or unsalted butter, divided
1 green pepper
2 ribs celery
2 pounds okra or 4 packages (8 ounces each) frozen
2 cups chopped onions
2 tablespoons chicken base
2 cups chopped plum tomatoes
1 tablespoon dried sweet basil
3 bay leaves
    Dash of cayenne, or to taste

Remove bones from chicken and cut meat into bite-size pieces. Sprinkle with hot sauce and salt and marinate for 15 minutes. Over medium heat, sauté chicken in 2 tablespoons of the oil until golden brown and set aside.

Chop green pepper, celery and okra into medium pieces. Sauté onions, green peppers and celery in remaining 2 tablespoons oil until tender. Add okra, chicken base, tomatoes, basil, bay leaves, cayenne, 2 quarts of water and sautéed chicken pieces. Simmer for about 15 minutes at low heat. This is where you may wish to be creative and add more cayenne, if your guests like that great "hot stuff."

Remove bay leaves. Serve over rice and top with freshly chopped green onions and parsley. Serve with a nice green salad, a glass of Chenin Blanc or Johannesburg Riesling wine.

~ Lagniappé ~

*For an extra kick, cut an all-beef sausage into pieces and sauté.
Put a few on top as a garnish—it's just super.*

Louisiana Dirty Rice

*This recipe earns its name from the appearance the rice takes on when
all ingredients are added. This is one of my favorite rice dishes.
It goes very well with any chicken or fish entree.
Try it with wild game for a real treat!*

*While the recipe calls for chicken livers and gizzards, one-half pound
ground turkey meat may be substituted. The turkey provides better flavor
and has much less cholesterol than the organ meat.*

Louisiana Dirty Rice will hold in the refrigerator for up to three days.

Yield: 4 servings

1/4	pound chicken livers
1/4	pound chicken gizzards
1/4	pound smoked beef sausage, optional
1/2	large green pepper
1/2	large white onion
1	tablespoon safflower oil
1/4	teaspoon black pepper
1	teaspoon chicken base
2	teaspoons sea salt
1/4	cup unsalted butter
4	cups cooked natural brown rice

Grind livers, gizzards, sausage (if desired), pepper and onion together in a food processor or meat grinder.

In a large pan over low heat, sauté the ground mixture in oil with black pepper, chicken base, sea salt and butter. Simmer for about 35 minutes.

Turn heat down very low and cook for another 35 minutes.

Mix in rice, continuing to simmer in the large pan. Heat the entire mixture long enough to allow flavors of meats and spices to permeate the rice, 10 to 15 minutes.

Serve as a side dish, garnished with fresh chopped parsley and green onions.

~ Lagniappé ~

*A delightful variation of this recipe is Seafood Dirty Rice.
Substitute 1/4 pound of your favorite fish and 1/4 pound shrimp
for the livers and gizzards, and grind with the other ingredients as above.*

Bayou Red Beans & Rice

Monday was the day for doing the laundry, and housewives didn't have time to cook. They'd put a pot of beans on the back burner and let it simmer all day while they tended to the family wash. At dinnertime they'd bring sausage out of the larder and serve the beans over rice with sausage and French bread. In keeping with this tradition, red beans and rice are served in restaurants all over Louisiana on Monday.

You can refrigerate this dish for up to three days if you add the turkey ham or for a week if you prepare the meatless version.

✤ 🄷 ★

Yield: 10 to 12 servings

4	cups dried red beans (kidney beans)
1	large white onion, finely chopped
2	tablespoons cumin
1	tablespoon garlic powder
1	tablespoon dried ground thyme
1	tablespoon dried oregano
1	teaspoon crushed dried red pepper
1/2	teaspoon cayenne, or to taste
1	tablespoon sea salt
1/2	pound turkey ham, diced, optional
5 to 6	cups cooked natural brown or white rice

Place beans in a large pot filled with water equal to 3 to 4 times the volume of beans; soak beans at room temperature for 3 to 4 hours. Overnight soaking is also good; however, I've found that 3 hours accomplishes the same effect. Pour off soaking water and replace with fresh water. Place pot over high heat and bring to a boil. Shut off heat, cover and let sit on burner for 10 minutes.

Stir in onion, cumin, garlic powder, thyme, oregano, red pepper and cayenne. Set heat on low and simmer for 30 to 45 minutes, or until beans reach the desired tenderness. About 10 minutes before beans have reached desired tenderness, add salt and turkey ham.

Remove the beans from heat and let sit for about 30 minutes. This gives all the wonderful seasonings time to "marry up." Remove 2 cups of beans and all of the liquid and blend in the blender until smooth. Return blended mixture to the bean pot. This makes for a richer, thicker bean stock.

To serve, place rice in center of plate, cover with red beans and garnish with freshly chopped parsley and green onions. Serve with a good quality smoked sausage, French bread and butter, and a nice green salad for a complete meal. A mellow red wine or beer makes it all fine!

Black-Eyed Peas

A strong southern tradition decrees that black-eyed peas served at the New Year's Eve meal will bring the family good luck throughout the new year. Traditional black-eyed pea recipes call for a pound of salt pork, but in these health-conscious times, addition of such gratuitous salt and fat is not a desired option. Happily, I've found that the black-eyed peas prepared without meat are as good or better than the traditional recipes. By the way, black-eyed peas aren't really peas at all—they're beans!

Great as a side dish or a main course served with sausage!

Black-Eyed Peas can be refrigerated for three to four days.

Yield: 8 cups

2 cups black-eyed peas (beans)	1 teaspoon crushed red pepper
1/2 cup chopped onion	1 cup turkey ham, optional
1/2 cup chopped green peppers	1 teaspoon black pepper
1/2 cup chopped celery	1 tablespoon sea salt
1 small clove garlic, chopped	1 teaspoon cayenne
1 bay leaf	Louisiana hot sauce, to taste
1 teaspoon white pepper	

Wash and drain the beans. Pick through and remove all the little stones, dirt and twigs. Soak overnight* in water equal to 3 times the volume of beans.

Drain beans and add fresh water. Bring beans to a boil and rapidly boil for 30 minutes; remove from heat. Add onions, green peppers, celery, garlic, bay leaf, white pepper, red pepper, turkey ham, if desired, and black pepper to the beans and stir to combine. Return mixture to heat, lower to simmer and cook until beans are tender, usually about 1 hour.

During the last 5 minutes of cooking time, add salt and cayenne and Louisiana hot sauce to taste.

Remove bay leave and serve Black-Eyed Peas over natural brown rice, garnished with a dash of cayenne and chopped green onions.

*I have found that if you can't soak the beans overnight, soaking them even 4 hours in room temperature water will help to reduce the cooking time.

Quick-soak method: If no soaking time is available, place washed and drained beans in a pot with water equal to 3 times the volume of beans. Bring to a rapid boil over medium high heat, and boil 10 minutes. Remove from heat and let "rest" for 10 minutes, return to heat and simmer for 45 minutes to 1 hour. Now you are ready to add vegetables and continue recipe above.

Bar-B-Que Beets

⚜ 𝕳 ★

Yield: 3¹/₂ cups

¹/₂ **medium onion, chopped**
  1 **tablespoon butter**
¹/₂ **cup Bayou Cajun Barbecue Sauce***
  1 **can (16 ounces) beets, drained**
¹/₈ **teaspoon ground cloves**

Sauté onions in butter over medium heat until translucent. Add barbecue sauce, beets and cloves. Cook over low heat until beets are heated, about 5 minutes, and serve. Or chill and serve as a salad.

* If Bayou Cajun Barbecue Sauce is unavailable in your area, substitute Chef Walter's Barbecue Sauce, recipe on page 100.

Cajun Style Bar-B-Que Cabbage

✣ 🜨 ★

Yield: 6 to 8 servings

1/2   large head cabbage
1/2   large sweet onion
  2   tablespoons unsalted butter
1/2   cup Bayou Cajun Barbecue Sauce*
      Salt to taste

Chop cabbage and onion into medium pieces. Melt butter in pot and add cabbage, onion and 1 cup water. Cook over medium heat for 5 minutes. Add barbeque sauce; lower heat and cook for 10 minutes. Salt to taste. Serve with or without rice.

* If Bayou Cajun Barbecue Sauce is unavailable in your area, substitute Chef Walter's Barbecue Sauce, recipe on page 100.

Blue Bayou Soufflé Potatoes

This recipe was developed to replace the twice-baked potato.
I really want you to try this recipe because it is a great one!

Soufflé Potatoes will keep in the refrigerator for up to five days,
or tightly wrapped in the freezer for one month.

Yield: 6 to 8 servings

2¹/₂	pounds red or white potatoes
¹/₂	cup (1 stick) unsalted butter, divided
³/₄	cup finely chopped white onions
¹/₄	cup grated Parmesan cheese
2	tablespoons finely chopped fresh parsley
	Dash of white pepper, or to taste
	Dash of sea salt, or to taste
¹/₄	cup grated Swiss cheese
¹/₄	cup grated Monterey Jack cheese
	Dash of paprika

Boil potatoes on high heat with skin on until just fork tender, about 30 minutes. Do not overcook! Rinse in cold water and grind in food processor or meat grinder.

Melt ¹/₄ cup of the butter over low heat in a sauté pan. Add onions and sauté until golden brown, about 25 minutes.

Melt the remaining ¹/₄ cup butter in another sauté pan over low heat or in a bowl in the microwave.

In a large mixing bowl, combine potatoes, onions, melted butter, Parmesan, parsley, white pepper and salt. Stir to blend. Mixture should be stiff but moist. If mixture appears too dry, add a little more melted butter or water.

Place mixture into a 9 x 12-inch baking pan. Combine Swiss and Monterey Jack cheeses, and sprinkle over potato mixture. Sprinkle paprika over top for color. Bake at 350 degrees until puffy and golden brown, 10 to 15 minutes.

~ Lagniappé ~

You can also mold the potato mixture by using a 1-cup measuring cup or large
ice cream scoop. Line pan with baking paper, and scoop the individual serving onto it.
Sprinkle cheeses and paprika over mounds, and bake at 325 degrees for 10 minutes.
Remember you are only reheating the potatoes and melting the cheese.
The individual portions will spread out of shape if overbaked.

Chef's Twice-Baked Potatoes

This is a great make-ahead side dish that can be molded into individual serving dishes and frozen until you are ready to use.

Yield: 5 to 6 servings

1/4	pound bacon
6	tablespoons unsalted butter, divided
1	cup minced onions
3/4	teaspoon sugar
21/2	pounds boiled or baked potatoes, cooled
1/2	tablespoon chicken base
1	teaspoon water
1	teaspoon white pepper
1	teaspoon salt

Lay bacon out in one layer on a baking pan. Cook in a preheated 400-degree oven until browned and crisp, 10 to 12 minutes. Drain and cool about 5 minutes. Crumble and set aside.

Melt 2 tablespoons of the butter in a sauté pan over low heat. Add onions and sauté until caramelized, stirring constantly. This process will take about 30 minutes; as cooking nears completion, slowly add up to 3/4 teaspoon sugar to enrich the caramelizing. Add remaining 4 tablespoons butter and heat until melted. Remove from heat and set aside.

Grind potatoes in a food processor or meat grinder and place the ground potatoes in a large mixing bowl. Dissolve chicken base in water, add to the potatoes and stir. One at a time, add white pepper, salt, onion mixture and bacon, mixing well after each addition.

Mold potato mixture into 8-ounce baking dishes. When ready to serve, reheat in a 375-degree oven for 20 to 25 minutes.

Entrees

All great accomplishments have simple beginnings

Bayou Stuffed Eggplant

Eggplant can be a most wonderful dish—I'm only surprised it's not served much more frequently. Try this one and see if you don't agree!

Stuffed Eggplant can be prepared ahead and stored up to four days in the refrigerator. I recommend that you make this a day or two ahead and refrigerate until time to serve—this makes it perfect to serve when entertaining, or to fix ahead for a hectic day when dinner has to be ready to heat and eat! If freezing, prepare eggplant without Creole Sauce. Place frozen eggplant in a 9x12-inch baking pan. Thaw 1/3 cup Master Creole Sauce per serving, pour over stuffed eggplant to serve. Bake 25 minutes in a 350-degree preheated oven at serving time.

⚜ ♨ ★

Yield: 12 servings

6 medium eggplants	3 bay leaves, optional
6 green onions	1 pound titi shrimp or crawfish tail
1/2 cup chopped white onions	meat, cooked
2 cloves garlic	1/2 pound lump crabmeat or cod,
1/4 cup chopped fresh parsley	cooked
1/2 cup (1 stick) unsalted butter	2 tablespoons Louisiana hot sauce
2 tablespoons dried thyme	2 cups bread crumbs
1/2 teaspoon black pepper	3 eggs
1/2 teaspoon cayenne	Paprika
1 teaspoon garlic powder	4 cups Master Creole Sauce,
1 tablespoon sea salt	recipe on page 105

Halve eggplants and place in salted boiling water in stock pot. Parboil until tender, about 30 minutes. Remove from pot and set aside to cool, about 30 minutes or until cool enough to handle. Spoon out eggplant pulp, taking care to keep the shells intact. Set shells aside, and cube the pulp into a mixing bowl.

In a food processor or meat grinder, grind together green onions, white onions, garlic and parsley. Melt butter in large pan and sauté ground ingredients over medium-low heat. While sautéing, stir in thyme, black pepper, cayenne, garlic powder, salt and bay leaves. Continue to cook until vegetables are very soft, about 25 minutes. Remove bay leaves.

Place sautéed mixture in a mixing bowl. Stir in cubed eggplant, cooked shrimp, lump crabmeat, Louisiana hot sauce, bread crumbs and eggs.

Arrange eggplant shells in baking pans. Fill each one with mixture, sprinkle with paprika and top each portion with Creole Sauce.

Bake in 350-degree oven for 15 to 25 minutes. Serve on a bed of shredded Romaine lettuce, accompanied by a fresh steamed vegetable.

~ Lagniappe ~

Whenever you use bay leaves in a recipe, be aware that they are a major culprit in choking incidents. So be sure to remove the bay leaves before serving the dish. For safety sake, you may consider putting leaves in a seasoning bag before adding to the recipe.

Jambalaya

Jambalaya is personal—a kind of signature dish for cooks who make it with any frequency. As with all of my recipes, the ingredients listed below are just suggestions—guidelines you can follow to get started in making jambalaya. Any or all of the following ingredients may be used (be creative—use your own imagination). Don't be afraid to experiment with different seasonings in this dish— develop a feeling, your own instinct, for cooking it. Combine your instincts with your family's preferences in the way of meats and seasonings to make your own personal jambalaya recipe a family tradition.

This recipe calls for three cups of cooked rice, which should be enough to serve six people. However, Jambalaya is like meatloaf, the more rice you add, the more you can serve with it. If you use more than the prescribed amount of rice, add enough Master Creole Sauce to make the rice mixture moist.

Yield: 6 servings

1/4	cup clarified unsalted butter
1/2	pound ham, cubed
1/2	pound shrimp, boiled and peeled
1/2	pound chicken, diced
1/2	pound spicy sausage
1/2	pound beef, diced
1/2	pound fish, any kind
1/2	pound chicken livers, or gizzards
3	cups cooked natural brown rice
3	cups Master Creole Sauce, recipe on page 105
1/4	cup shredded cheddar cheese, optional

In the clarified butter over low heat, sauté ham, shrimp, chicken, sausage, beef, fish and chicken livers. Stirring frequently, sauté until raw ingredients are cooked and others are well heated, about 20 to 25 minutes.

In a large bowl, combine sautéed mixture with rice and Creole Sauce. Transfer to 12-ounce casserole dishes and place in preheated 300-degree oven for 10 to 15 minutes.

If desired, top with shredded cheddar cheese and return to oven for the last 3 minutes of baking time. Serve immediately.

Shrimp Jambalaya

⚜ 出 ★

Yield: 5 to 6 servings

1	pound peeled, deveined shrimp (any size)
1/4	cup safflower oil
1	cup chopped onions
1/2	cup chopped celery
1/2	cup chopped bell pepper
4	cloves garlic, minced
2	tablespoons tomato paste
1	teaspoon dried thyme
1	teaspoon dried oregano
	Dash of salt, or to taste
	Dash of white pepper, or to taste
	Dash of cayenne, or to taste
1	teaspoon sugar
2	tablespoons cornstarch
4	cups natural brown rice, cooked

Chop shrimp and set aside.

Heat oil in a heavy pot over medium heat. Add onions, celery, bell pepper and garlic. Cook uncovered, stirring frequently, until onions are tender and translucent, about 20 minutes.

Add tomato paste, and continue to cook, stirring constantly, for 15 minutes. Stir in 1 1/2 cups water. Season mixture with thyme, oregano, salt, white pepper and cayenne. Add sugar and cook uncovered, stirring occasionally, for about 40 minutes, or until oil floats to the top.

Add shrimp and continue to cook and stir for another 20 minutes.

Dissolve cornstarch in 1/2 cup water and add to the mixture, cooking for another 5 minutes. Mix in the rice and leave on heat 3 to 5 minutes, or until rice is heated thoroughly. Spoon into casserole dishes. Garnish with chopped green onions and parsley.

Shrimp Étouffée

✣ ♨ ★

Yield: 2 servings

16 shrimp (16 to 20 or 21 to 25 count)
1 teaspoon plus dash of sea salt
2 tablespoons plus 1 1/2 teaspoons
   Louisiana hot sauce, divided
1/2 cup (1 stick) unsalted butter
3 cups diced white onion
1 1/2 cups diced green pepper
3/4 cup diced celery
1 tablespoon chopped parsley
1 1/2 teaspoons dried thyme
1 1/2 teaspoons Worcestershire sauce
1 teaspoon crushed red pepper
Dash of cayenne
Dash of white pepper
1 tablespoon whole wheat flour

Peel shrimp. Marinate in 1 teaspoon of the salt and 2 tablespoons of the hot sauce for about 10 minutes.

Melt butter over low heat in a large pan. Stir in onion, green pepper, celery, parsley, thyme, Worcestershire sauce, remaining 1 1/2 teaspoons hot sauce, red pepper, cayenne, white pepper and dash of sea salt. Turn heat up to medium and cook until the vegetables start to soften and begin to stick to the bottom of the pan, 15 to 20 minutes. Keep stirring, gently scraping the bottom of the pan to keep vegetables from burning.

Add 1/2 cup water to deglaze pan, stirring thoroughly to loosen everything on the bottom. Cook 2 to 3 minutes.

Add flour and shrimp to the mixture. Simmer until shrimp are tender and mixture is thickened, about 10 minutes.

Serve over a bed of brown rice, with French bread and a green salad.

Louisiana Stuffed Shrimp

Traditional Louisiana stuffed shrimp are deep-fried.
When done properly, they are marvelous.
However, even though the following recipe could be dipped in an egg wash,
then rolled in a breading and deep-fried, I prefer to bake them in a casserole dish.
To me, shrimp is delicate and should be treated as such!

Yield: 4 servings as an entree, 8 as an appetizer

6	green onions	1/8	teaspoon ground allspice
1	rib celery	1	tablespoon Louisiana hot sauce
1/2	cup unsalted butter, divided	3/4	cup white wine, divided
1/2	pound lump crabmeat or cod	1	egg
2	tablespoons chopped fresh parsley	1	cup bread crumbs
1	tablespoon dried thyme	2	pounds (21 to 25 count) shrimp
1	teaspoon salt		Dash of paprika

Chop green onions and dice celery. Over low heat, melt 1/4 cup of the butter until slightly browned. Add green onions and celery. Sauté until celery is tender and onions are translucent, about 15 minutes. Add cod (if substituting for crabmeat), parsley, thyme, salt, allspice, hot sauce and 1/2 cup of the wine. Simmer for 5 minutes.

Add lump crabmeat (if using this ingredient), egg and bread crumbs and mix well. Remove from heat and allow mixture to "rest" while preparing the shrimp.

Peel shrimp, leaving tail on. Make an incision in the meat of the shrimp, running lengthwise, starting at the tail. Just form a v-shaped pocket to hold stuffing. DO NOT CUT ALL THE WAY THROUGH.

Take teaspoon-size balls of the stuffing mixture and place in the incision made in the shrimp. Lap tail over the ball. Stand shrimp up for baking (place meat end down, tail up), filling baking dish with stuffed shrimp.

Melt remaining 1/4 cup butter. Pour butter and remaining 1/4 cup wine over the shrimp and sprinkle with paprika. Bake at 375 degrees until golden brown, 12 to 15 minutes.

~ Lagniappe ~

Top shrimp with Bearnaise Sauce (recipe on page 107) before serving for a wonderful finishing touch! Serve with French bread, white wine and a green salad. SUPER!

Barbecued Shrimp

*This recipe is just too good to describe. It's not just a meal—
it's a delightful dining experience! It is a recipe using the
Blended Flavors Barbecue Mixture, recipe on page 111.*

Yield: 1 serving as an entree, 2 as an appetizer

1/4	**cup diced onions**
8 to 10	**shrimp (15 to 20 count)**
2	**teaspoons Blended Flavors Mixture, recipe on page 111**
2	**tablespoons white wine**
2	**tablespoons safflower oil**
1	**small wedge of lemon**
1	**small clove garlic**

Place onions on bottom of a 12-ounce casserole dish. Layer shrimp over onions
and sprinkle flavors mixture on top.

Pour wine and oil over the seasonings. Squeeze lemon juice from wedge over oil,
and place garlic clove in casserole. Bake at 400 degrees for 25 to 30 minutes, or until
golden brown.

Serve with a side dish of natural brown rice and garnish with chopped green
onion. French bread is a must with this dish—to soak up the luscious sauce.

Sweet Basil Shrimp

*This recipe was created in honor of my mother-in-law,
Mrs. Rita Johnson, a wonderful person.
She loves shrimp and asked me to make her a dish "on the mild side."*

*In this recipe, the shrimp are first sautéed and then allowed to steep for five minutes.
While other methods may overcook the shrimp, leaving them rubbery,
this method allows the shrimp to cook to perfection every time.*

Yield: 1 serving as an entree, 2 as an appetizer

8   large (21 to 25 count) shrimp, peeled
    Dash of Louisiana hot sauce
    Dash of sea salt
3   tablespoons unsalted butter
1/4 cup white wine (chablis preferred)
1   teaspoon dried sweet basil leaves or 2 teaspoons fresh

Marinate shrimp in Louisiana hot sauce and salt for 10 minutes.

Over low heat, melt butter in sauté pan until slightly browned. Add shrimp, wine and basil and cook 2 to 3 minutes, until shrimp turn pink. Remove from heat; cover and let steep for 5 minutes.

Return to heat briefly before serving. Serve over hot rice with French bread and a glass of dry or semi-sweet white wine.

Shrimp De Jonghe

I first had Shrimp De Jonghe years ago in Chicago and loved it.
After that I had it many times, in almost as many different ways.
It was so good I worked on developing my own recipe for it, which I am proud
to serve in my restaurant. I'm sure you'll be equally proud to put it on your table.
Don't forget to add your own personal touches as you prepare this.

✤ 片 ★

Yield: 4 servings as an entree, 8 as an appetizer

2   pounds (16 to 20 count) shrimp, peeled
    Master Garlic Butter Supreme, recipe on page 110
1   cup wine, or more (chablis preferred)
1/2 cup bread crumbs, or more

Lay shrimp on bottom of a 1 1/2-quart baking dish. Slice butter in medallions of desired thickness: thin for a lower-fat version, thick for a richer recipe. Place medallions on shrimp.

Pour wine into baking dish, enough to completely submerge shrimp. Sprinkle coating of bread crumbs over shrimp.

Place in preheated 400-degree oven and bake until rim of dish is golden brown, 25 to 30 minutes. Take care not to overcook.

Serve over natural brown rice or angel hair pasta with French bread and a green salad.

~ Lagniappe ~

This dish is traditionally served over rice or pasta,
but if you want to go for something really different,
ladle the mixture over some fresh, warm French or Italian bread.
Folks just love to dip the bread into the De Jonghe sauce—dynamite!
A side of crisp green salad, and however you've served the De Jonghe,
it's a repast fit for a king!

Shrimp Victoria (for Two)

*This recipe is considered just good down-home cookin' in Louisiana.
It's an old Cajun favorite (and mine too!) regarded more as gourmet fare
in the rest of the world. It certainly is a favorite at the Blue Bayou Inn!*

Yield: 2 servings as an entree, 4 as an appetizer

 16 shrimp (15 to 20 count)
 1/4 cup Louisiana hot sauce
  1 teaspoon sea salt
 1/2 cup (1 stick) unsalted butter or safflower oil
 1/2 cup chopped green onions
  1 clove garlic, minced, or 1 teaspoon garlic salt
  2 tablespoons finely chopped fresh parsley
  1 cup sliced fresh mushrooms
 1/2 cup white wine (chablis preferred)
  1 tablespoon whole wheat pastry flour
 1/4 to 1/2 cup sour cream

Marinate shrimp in hot sauce and sea salt for 5 minutes.

In a large sauté pan over low heat, melt butter until slightly browned (do not substitute margarine in this recipe). Add green onions and sauté for 1 minute. Add garlic, parsley and mushrooms, sautéing until mushrooms start to turn brown.

Add shrimp and white wine. Sauté until shrimp turn pink, about 5 minutes. Stir in flour.

Reduce heat to simmer, continuing to stir, and cook until sauce thickens, about 10 minutes. Remove from heat and let steep about 5 minutes. Just before serving, add sour cream and return to low heat until the mixture bubbles.

Serve immediately. Ladle over your choice of potatoes, natural brown rice, or pasta and top with chopped green onions.

~ Lagniappé ~

*Always buy shrimp in the shell.
It's the best way to buy it and will give you the best flavor.*

Crawfish

Crawfish are very important to Louisiana cookery. Over the years, crawfish farms have developed, and millions—yes, millions—of pounds of crawfish are produced each year. About 90 percent of that harvest is consumed in Louisiana itself.

✣ ㄆ ★

Purging Crawfish

The most important part of preparing crawfish is to purge them before cooking. Purging thoroughly cleans the exterior and interior (mud track) of the crawfish. Follow these instructions exactly because proper purging plays a big part in enabling you to bring out the best flavor of the crawfish itself.

To purge, place live crawfish in enough cold water to submerge them. Add 1 cup salt and let crawfish soak for 15 minutes.

After soaking, pour off water, fill with clean cold water, and repeat procedure.

After purging twice, crawfish are ready to cook.

✣ ㄆ ★

Boiling Crawfish

Yield: 10 pounds whole crawfish will produce 1 pound tail meat

     10   pounds purged crawfish, live
      1   bag shrimp & crawfish boil seasoning,
            use commercial mix or try recipe on page 78
      1   lemon, halved
      2   small onions
      2   stalks celery, coarsely chopped
    1/2   cup salt
    1/2   teaspoon cayenne

Fill a 20-quart pot halfway with water. Place seasoning bag in water with lemon, onions, celery, salt and cayenne.

Bring water to a rapid boil, then add live crawfish. Cook until water returns to a boil; crawfish will turn red. Simmer for 5 minutes, then remove from heat. Remove crawfish from pot and ice down immediately to avoid overcooking. Once crawfish are cooled, peel to yield 1 pound tail meat. The crawfish are now ready to eat or be used in another recipe.

Crawfish/Shrimp/Crab Boil Spice Mix

⚜ ⨆ ★

1	cup salt
1/2	teaspoon dry mustard
1	teaspoon crushed red pepper
1	teaspoon dill seed
3	laurel leaves
1	teaspoon coriander seed
1	teaspoon crushed dried thyme
1	teaspoon black pepper
1	teaspoon crushed allspice
1	teaspoon crushed cloves

Place all ingredients in a seasoning bag or place on a piece of cloth and tie the edges to form a pouch.

A similar mix is available in better specialty stores. There is also a liquid boil seasoning available; however, if the crawfish is to be used in another recipe, don't use it—the liquid form has too strong a flavor and will overpower your recipe.

Crab Boil

If you wish to make a meal of plain boiled crawfish,
follow the instructions above, adding corn on the cob, red potatoes and
more onions along with the spices and herbs.

After removing from heat, let stand for 10 minutes, then serve.
Serve with hot sauce or clarified butter, cocktail sauce and crackers,
or just peel and save the meat for making other dishes.

Bayou Crawfish Étouffée—Creamy

Étouffée, pronounced A-Too-Fay, is Cajun for "smothered in sauce."

✤ Ħ ★

Yield: 4 to 6 servings

        10 pounds live crawfish
        1/4 cup plus 2/3 cup unsalted butter, divided
         3 cups finely chopped white onions
        1/4 cup finely chopped fresh parsley
        2/3 cup whole wheat pastry or unbleached flour
         2 cups half-and-half
         1 cup milk
       11/2 cups white wine
        1/2 teaspoon garlic salt
         6 tablespoons tomato paste
         2 dashes of Tabasco
             Dash of sea salt, or to taste

Purge and boil crawfish according to instructions on page 77. This process will yield approximately 1 pound crawfish tail meat.

Over low heat, melt 1/4 cup of the butter and sauté onions and parsley until onions are translucent, about 20 minutes.

In a large pan, melt remaining 2/3 cup of the butter over low heat. While continuing to heat, slowly whisk in flour to make a light roux (page 51). As soon as the roux begins to thicken, add half-and-half and milk and continue to cook, stirring constantly until the sauce is rich and creamy, about 30 minutes.

Stir wine into cream sauce; continue to simmer for another 10 minutes, stirring frequently. At this point, the sauce may be transferred to a double boiler to prevent burning.

Add cooked crawfish tails, sautéed onions and parsley, garlic salt, tomato paste, Tabasco and salt. Simmer another 10 minutes, stirring frequently to avoid burning the sauce—watch carefully during this process.

Serve over rice, accompanied by a semi-dry white wine, if you wish.

Crawfish Étouffée—Spicy

✦ ⵙ ★

Yield: 6 to 8 servings

10	pounds live crawfish
1	cup (2 sticks) unsalted butter
6	cups finely chopped onions
3	cups chopped green pepper
1½	cups finely chopped celery
2	tablespoons finely chopped parsley
1	tablespoon dried sweet basil
1	tablespoon Worcestershire sauce
1	tablespoon Louisiana hot sauce
1	tablespoon sea salt
1	teaspoon cayenne
½	teaspoon white pepper
½	teaspoon crushed red pepper
6	tablespoons tomato paste
2	tablespoons whole wheat pastry or unbleached flour

Purge and boil crawfish according to instructions on page 77. This process will yield approximately 1 pound crawfish tail meat.

Melt butter over low heat in a large pan. Add onions, green pepper, celery, parsley, sweet basil, Worcestershire sauce, hot sauce, sea salt, cayenne, white pepper and red pepper. Stir to combine and turn heat up to medium. Cook until vegetables start to soften and begin to stick to the bottom of the pan, 15 to 20 minutes. Keep stirring, gently scraping the bottom of the pan to keep vegetables from burning.

Deglaze pan by adding 2 cups water; stir thoroughly to loosen everything on the bottom. Cook 2 to 3 minutes.

Stir in tomato paste, flour and crawfish tail meat and simmer until thickened, about 10 minutes.

Serve over cooked natural brown rice.

Crabmeat Au Gratin

*Lump crabmeat is highly prized in New Orleans cuisine because
it is so wonderful tasting. It's expensive, too, as it takes the meat from many crabs
to make a pound. Try this recipe for a true southern delicacy. Traditionally it is served
at Sunday Brunch, but you're sure to get enthusiastic approval any time
you present this rich and tantalizing dish.*

Yield: 4 servings as an entree, 8 to 12 as an appetizer

1	cup white wine
2	cups Mornay Sauce, recipe on page 108
1	pound lump crabmeat
1/2	cup bread crumbs
	Dash of paprika

Combine wine and Mornay Sauce. Stir in crabmeat.

Place mixture in 1½-quart casserole dish, top with bread crumbs and a dash or two of paprika. Bake uncovered in preheated 350-degree oven until edges turn light brown, 10 to 15 minutes.

Serve with green salad, French bread and semi-dry white wine. Simple and just great!

Oyster Loaf Porboy "The Peacemaker"

Tradition has it that when a New Orleans husband spent the night drinking with friends in the French Quarter, "The Peacemaker" (Oyster Loaf Porboy) was brought home and was tossed inside the doorway before he entered. The sandwich was such a delectable treat that all was forgiven by the wife upon discovery of the palatable peace offering. Ha! Ha! I haven't tested THAT particular theory for myself; however, it really IS a great offering, whether you need to "make peace" or just please your family or guests.

While the recipe calls for corn flour, unbleached or whole wheat flour may be substituted, or use a combination.

✤ Ⱨ ★

Yield: 2 servings

2 loaves French or Italian bread (6 to 8 inches each)	2 eggs, slightly beaten
1/4 cup unsalted butter, melted	1/2 cup evaporated milk
1 pint oysters, or 12 shucked	1/4 cup safflower oil for frying
1 tablespoon Louisiana hot sauce	1/2 cup tartar sauce, optional
Dash plus 1/2 teaspoon sea salt	1/2 cup cocktail sauce, optional
1/2 teaspoon white pepper	1/4 cup shredded lettuce
1/4 teaspoon cayenne	1 tomato, sliced
1 cup unsifted corn flour	1 dill pickle, sliced thin

Slice loaves of bread in half horizontally. Scoop out both sides of the soft white inner portions, giving the crusts the appearance of boatlike shells. Coat the inside of the bread shells with melted butter. Place them in a preheated 350-degree oven and bake until the insides are crisp and golden brown, 10 to 15 minutes.

Marinate oysters in hot sauce and a dash of salt for 5 minutes. In a separate bowl, combine 1/2 teaspoon salt, white pepper, cayenne and corn flour.

Whip together eggs and evaporated milk, and dip oysters into this egg wash. Dredge coated oysters in the corn flour mixture and fry in 2 inches of cooking oil heated to 375 degrees until golden brown, 1 to 2 minutes or until they float.

Spread tartar or cocktail sauce on both sides of each loaf, then layer one side of each with shredded lettuce and the other with tomatoes and pickle slices.

Nestle 6 fried oysters on each lettuce bed, cover with other half and serve with a nice cooled beer—terrific!

Catfish Courtboullion

Courtboullion (coo-be-yon) is a great dish from Cajun Country.
Any kind of small white fish can be used. Traditionally a dark roux
(about one-half cup) is added with the fish to the rest of the sauce.
I like it without the dark roux, personally, but you should try it both ways.

Here again is a recipe that should challenge your imagination. Try other types of fish
or add shrimp to give it a wonderful new character. Be creative—wow!

Yield: 2 servings as an entree, 4 as an appetizer

1	large green pepper
4	green onions
1	rib celery
1	large tomato
1/2	pound (31 to 35 count) peeled shrimp
1	tablespoon chopped fresh parsley
1	teaspoon dried thyme
1	teaspoon dried sweet basil
	Dash of sea salt, or to taste
1	teaspoon hot sauce
	Dash of white pepper
	Dash of cayenne
1	pound catfish, cut into bite-size pieces

Cut green pepper into strips and halve. Cut onions and celery into strips 1 1/2 inches long. Dice tomato into bite-size pieces. In a large stock pot, combine shrimp, green pepper, onion, celery, tomato, 1 1/2 quarts water, parsley, thyme, basil, salt, hot sauce, white pepper and cayenne. Bring mixture to a boil over medium heat.

Reduce heat and simmer for 10 minutes. Taste for flavor.

Add catfish and simmer until fish is tender, 5 to 7 minutes. Don't overcook!

Serve in a bowl, garnished with chopped green onion and parsley, with a side dish of steamed rice, French bread and butter.

Catfish Creole

✦ Ħ ★

Yield: 2 servings as an entree, 4 as an appetizer

1   pound catfish fillets (fillets of 3 to 6 ounces each)
1   cup Master Creole Sauce, page 105

Place fillets in a 9 x 12-inch baking pan. Pour Master Creole Sauce over fillets to cover them completely, using more sauce if necessary.

Bake uncovered at 325 degrees for 25 minutes or until fillets are tender.

Serve Catfish Creole on a bed of rice. A light salad, French bread and, of course, a glass of dry white wine are the perfect complements to this dish.

Blackened Catfish

Sometimes it's smart to take advantage of the convenience of a commercial mix, especially when you will still have the opportunity to add your own very special magic. Paul Prudhomme is "the man" when it comes to blackening foods— he is a famous Louisiana chef who invented the process in the late 1970's. If you use a commercial mix, I highly recommend his excellent product. If you wish to venture out on your own, see my Blackened Spice Mixture recipe on page 112.

The secret to success for Blackened Catfish (and other "blackened" recipes for that matter) is to use very high heat—you can't have the pan too hot for this recipe. But remember, there are inherent problems in cooking at high temperatures. First, always use a very heavy pan—non-stick pans cannot endure this kind of cooking. I recommend a heavy cast-iron pan if it is available; they really are the best. Secondly, it is critical to prepare this recipe in a well-ventilated situation—under a hooded vent or out-of-doors on a propane stove.

You can control the "heat" of blackened food simply by adjusting the amount of spice mixture you coat it with. Start out with a light coating sprinkled on each side, and if it's not hot enough to suit your family, use more next time. I also recommend cooking the fillets one at a time to keep careful control over the cooking process, at least until cooking blackened food has become "second nature."

⚜ Ħ ★

Yield: 6 servings

1½ cups (3 sticks) unsalted butter
6 catfish fillets (5 to 7 ounces each), fresh or thawed
3 tablespoons Blackened Spice Mixture, page 112, or use a good commercial mixture

Melt butter and set it aside.

Heat a large cast-iron skillet over very high heat for about 10 minutes—don't worry, you can't have the pan too hot for this recipe.

Sprinkle blackened spice mixture on both sides of each fillet. Place fillets on hot skillet and pour 1 teaspoon melted butter on top of the fillet as it is placed in the pan. Be very careful doing this since the butter can flame up over such high heat.

Cook fillets uncovered until the underside is charred, about 2 minutes, but this can vary according to the thickness of the fillet. When done on one side, turn fish over, pouring 1 teaspoon melted butter over fillet as it is turned. It will take almost another 2 minutes to complete cooking.

Serve each fillet hot, preferably on a heated platter, accompanied by melted butter.

Snapper Creole

✤ 𝕳 ★

Yield: 8 servings

1	red snapper (4 to 4 1/2 pounds), dressed
1/2	cup lime juice
1/2	teaspoon salt
1/2	teaspoon pepper
2	cups Master Creole Sauce, recipe on page 105
2	tablespoons chopped stuffed green olives
1	teaspoon capers
1/2	teaspoon cilantro
1	teaspoon sugar
1	tablespoon red wine vinegar
2	tablespoons olive oil
1	cup chopped onion
2	cloves garlic, finely chopped

Marinate snapper in lime juice, salt and pepper while preparing other ingredients.

Put Master Creole Sauce in a mixing bowl, and stir in olives, capers, cilantro, sugar and vinegar. Set aside.

In olive oil over medium heat, sauté onions and garlic until onions are tender and translucent, about 20 minutes. Set aside.

Brush one side of the snapper with additional olive oil, and place the snapper that side down into a baking dish. Fill cavity of fish with onions and garlic. Pour the Master Creole Sauce mixture over the fish. Bake in preheated 350-degree oven for 1 hour.

Garnish with slivered almonds and serve on a warmed platter with a side dish of brown rice and a loaf of French bread and butter.

Alligator Étouffée

*Alligator was taken off the endangered species list in the past few years.
Now good farming procedures have made more and more domestically
raised alligator available every year.*

Alligator Étouffée freezes well, or you can refrigerate it for three to four days.

Yield: 2 to 4 servings

1 1/4	pounds alligator meat, dark (body) or light (tail meat) with bones if available	1	can (26-ounces) crushed tomatoes
1/2	tablespoon sea salt	1/4	cup Worcestershire sauce
1/2	cup vegetable oil	2	tablespoons beef base
1/2	cup whole wheat pastry flour	1/8	teaspoon ground allspice
1/2	large onion, chopped medium	1/8	teaspoon cayenne
2	tablespoons chopped celery	1/4	teaspoon crushed red pepper
2	medium cloves garlic, chopped fine	1/4	teaspoon black pepper
2 to 3	carrots, chopped medium	3/4	tablespoon thyme
1/2	cup finely chopped parsley	1	bay leaf
		1	cup sherry

Place alligator meat in stock pot with salt and 6 cups water. Bring to a boil, lower heat to simmer and cook until tender, about 1 hour. Remove meat from pot and set aside to cool, about 15 to 20 minutes. Save alligator stock; without it this dish never comes to life! Cut cooled meat into cubes; discard bones.

Using flour and oil, prepare a dark roux (page 51). When the roux has achieved a rich dark color, add onions, celery, garlic, carrots and parsley. Simmer until vegetables are tender and onions are translucent, about 20 minutes.

Place roux mixture into large pot and add tomatoes, Worcestershire sauce, beef base, allspice, cayenne, red pepper, black pepper, thyme, bay leaf, sherry and half of the alligator stock.

Simmer for 15 minutes. If étouffée is thicker in consistency than you wish (it should be the consistency of pudding), gradually add more of the alligator stock until the mixture thins to the desired consistency. Discard remaining stock or save for use in other recipes. Remove bay leaf and check for seasoning.

Serve with pasta or natural brown rice. Garnish with freshly chopped green onion and parsley and serve with French bread and butter.

Chicken Étouffée

Pronounced A-Too-Fay, étouffée is Cajun French for "smothered in sauce."
You'll probably find a number of chicken étouffée recipes.
I like chicken myself so I worked on this one to get it exactly to my liking.
Don't be afraid to personalize it to YOUR own taste, but if you don't,
I think you'll probably like this one just the way it is.

This can be frozen, in portions, or held in the refrigerator for up to four days.

✤ ൯ ★

Yield: 4 servings

1	chicken (3 to 3 1/2 pounds)	2	tablespoons dried sweet basil
1	tablespoon Louisiana hot sauce	2	tablespoons chopped fresh parsley
1	tablespoon sea salt	1	tablespoon minced garlic
1/4	cup clarified butter, divided		Dash of cayenne
6	cups diced white onions	1	cup white wine (chablis preferred)
3	cups diced green peppers	2	tablespoons whole wheat flour
1 1/2	cups diced celery		

Remove skin and fat from chicken and reserve. Bone chicken and cut meat into bite-size pieces. Place chicken pieces in a dish and sprinkle with hot sauce and salt. Leave it to marinate about 5 minutes.

Place reserved chicken fat and skin into a heavy skillet over medium heat and sauté until skin is golden brown, 5 to 7 minutes. Discard skin. Remove all but 2 tablespoons of the melted chicken fat (adding more if needed). Place chicken pieces into remaining fat and cook to golden brown, about 6 minutes. Set aside.

In another heavy skillet, over medium-low heat, melt butter and add onions, green pepper, celery, basil, parsley, garlic and cayenne. Sauté until ingredients are actually sticking to the bottom of the pan, about 20 minutes. Mix and let sticking occur two more times. Remove from heat. This procedure actually extracts and forces the flavors of the vegetables into the étouffée.

Add 1/4 cup water to deglaze pan, stirring thoroughly to loosen everything on the bottom. Continue to cook 2 to 3 minutes.

Stir in wine, flour, 3/4 cup water and chicken. Turn heat to low and simmer for 10 to 15 minutes, stirring constantly, until thickened. Check for salt and add if needed.

Serve over rice and sprinkle with fresh chopped green onions and parsley.

~ Lagniappé ~

For a wonderful side dish, mix up corn, okra and tomato—
use your imagination to season this mix to give it your personal touch!
For a change of pace, serve Chicken Étouffée over pasta!

Chicken De Jonghe

This is a great recipe to prepare for a luncheon.
Serve with salad and make it an afternoon repast they won't soon forget!

Yield: 4 servings

4   chicken breasts, skinless
1/4 cup Louisiana hot sauce
     Dash of sea salt, or to taste
8   medallions Master Garlic Butter Supreme,
       recipe on page 110, cut 1/4-inch thick
1/2 cup bread crumbs
2   cups white wine

Arrange chicken breast in pan or casserole. Rub hot sauce and a pinch of sea salt into each breast. Lay 2 medallions of garlic butter on top of each breast. Sprinkle with bread crumbs.

Add wine to fill pan 3/4 of the way up the breasts. Bake in oven preheated to 400 degrees until golden brown, 25 to 30 minutes.

Arrange rice or pasta in a circle on the plate and place chicken breast in the center. Garnish with a sprinkle of parsley. French or Italian bread with this is a must!

Chicken Cranberria

Each year, one of the local cranberry growers generously presents me with fresh cranberries to use in the restaurant. It seemed only fitting, in honor of his generosity, and the fact that my restaurant is in the heart of some of the finest cranberry country in the world, that I should create special dishes using cranberries. This recipe is one of my favorites, because I truly love chicken.

I list Ocean Spray cranberry juice by its brand name for a reason. I know they have wonderful cranberry products because they buy the cranberries grown with such loving care by my friends and neighbors here in Manitowish Waters. Accompany Chicken Cranberria with my wonderful fresh cranberry sauce, recipe on page 98.

This recipe calls for a larger chicken because it will be totally skinned. However, a smaller chicken will work just as well.

Yield: 4 servings

1   chicken (3 to 3 1/2 pounds)
2   cups Ocean Spray Cranberry Juice
2   tablespoons Louisiana hot sauce
    Dash of salt

Remove the wings from the chicken, and cut bird in half. Remove skin from both halves. Quarter-cut the chicken, and separate the legs from thighs.

Place all chicken pieces into a stainless steel bowl and cover with cranberry juice. Marinate in refrigerator for at least 6 hours or overnight, turning the pieces once.

Place chicken pieces in baking pan. Rub lightly with hot sauce and salt to taste. Pour cranberry juice marinade over chicken and cover pan.

Bake in 350-degree oven about 40 minutes or until chicken is done. Uncover pan for the last 10 minutes of cooking time to give chicken a nice brown color.

Serve over a bed of natural brown rice, pouring the drippings from the pan over the chicken and rice. Serve North/South Cranberry Sauce, page 98, on the side.

Chicken Cumin

This recipe is one of my creations. I worked this up because I love the taste of cumin...

✤ ⵀ ★

Yield: 4 servings as an entree, 8 as an appetizer

1 chicken (3 to 3½ pounds), boned
¼ cup Louisiana hot sauce, or to taste
1 teaspoon sea salt, or to taste
¼ cup clarified unsalted butter or safflower oil
2 tablespoons ground cumin
2 large onions, diced

Cut chicken into bite-size pieces. Combine hot sauce and salt. Coat chicken pieces with the mixture.

Heat clarified butter on medium in sauté pan. Place chicken in hot butter. Brown on one side, sprinkle with cumin and turn chicken.

Add onions and sauté on medium-low heat until chicken and onions are tender and golden brown, 3 to 5 minutes.

Serve over hot steamed rice with a garnish of green onions and fresh chopped parsley.

Chicken Pontalba

The basic recipe for this delightful dish was created by a New Orleans chef in 1899 for a dinner in honor of an architect named Pontalba who had designed the first apartment complex in the country.

⚜ ♓ ★

Yield: 4 servings

2	large chicken breasts, cut in half, skin removed
2	tablespoons Louisiana hot sauce
	Dash of sea salt
1/2	cup clarified unsalted butter or safflower oil, divided
2	cups diced potatoes, 1/2-inch cubes
1 1/2	cups thinly sliced green onion
2	cups fresh sliced mushrooms
1	cup diced turkey ham, 1/2-inch cubes
1 1/2	cups dry white wine (chablis preferred)
1	cup Bearnaise Sauce, recipe on page 107

Rub chicken with hot sauce and salt, and allow to marinate for 10 minutes.

Preheat a sauté pan over low heat. Pour in 1/4 cup of the butter and add potatoes. Sauté until potatoes are golden brown, 5 to 7 minutes. Add green onions, mushrooms, turkey ham and wine. Salt to taste and continue to sauté over medium-low heat for about 10 minutes more.

Heat another sauté pan, placing enough of the remaining clarified butter in the pan to coat the bottom. Add chicken, and sauté until golden brown, 5 to 7 minutes. Turn and finish cooking an additional 5 to 7 minutes.

Place potato mixture on plate, put a piece of chicken in center of mixture and top with Bearnaise Sauce. Sprinkle with parsley and paprika.

Stuffed Cornish Hen

⚜ ♙ ★

Yield: 2 servings

1/2	tablespoon clarified butter
3	cups julienne cut red potatoes
3	cups finely diced white onions
11/2	cups julienne cut carrots
3/4	cup finely diced celery
1	teaspoon plus a dash salt, divided
3/4	tablespoon plus 1/4 cup Louisiana hot sauce
3/4	tablespoon ground cumin
1/2	tablespoon finely chopped fresh parsley
2	Rock Cornish hens (1 pound each)
1	can (10 ounces) whole cranberry sauce
1/2	cup praline liqueur
2	tablespoons brown sugar
1/2	cup alfalfa sprouts or shredded romaine lettuce
6	pecan halves

Heat clarified butter over low heat in a large sauté pan. Add potatoes, onions, carrots and celery. Sauté, stirring frequently, until nearly tender, 15 to 20 minutes.

Add 1 teaspoon salt, 3/4 tablespoon of the hot sauce and cumin; sauté until vegetables are tender and onions become translucent, another 5 to 10 minutes. Remove from heat. Stir in parsley and let rest for 5 minutes.

Rub hens inside and out with remaining 1/4 cup Louisiana hot sauce. Add a dash of salt to inside of hen and stuff with sautéed vegetable mixture.

Place hens in pan and bake uncovered in 400-degree oven for 40 minutes. Hens will be done when a leg moves up and down easily when gently prodded with a utensil or protected hand.

Meanwhile, make Praline Cranberry Sauce. Pour cranberry sauce into a saucepan, stirring and cutting whole berries to break them down into small pieces. Add liqueur and brown sugar and simmer on low heat for 10 minutes, stirring frequently to check for sticking.

Swirl about half of the Praline Cranberry Sauce in a circle on each of two serving platters, retaining a little of the sauce for garnish. Arrange either alfalfa sprouts or shredded romaine lettuce on the edge of the platter, around the sauce. Place hen head first on the platter over the sauce. Garnish with the reserved sauce and top with 3 pecan halves on each bird.

Roast Duck

Roast duck is one of my all-time favorite dishes. I have a hard time satisfying my craving for roast duck unless I cook it myself! The following recipes came about after two years of intensive research. As I look back now, it was worth every minute and every bit of trouble I went through to come up with it. You'll agree once you've tried it!

One of the biggest mistakes I see people making with roast duck is that they don't let the duck cook until it is done! I've had some duck finish after only 2 hours and 15 minutes. Then, two days later, same oven, same everything—I've had the same size duck take 3 and a half hours to cook. Why? Atmospheric pressure is usually the culprit—it can dramatically affect the time it takes to cook. An older bird will also require a longer cooking time.

Yield: 2 servings

1 duck (4 1/2 to 5 pounds), split in half	1 teaspoon paprika
1/4 cup Louisiana hot sauce	1 teaspoon dried sweet basil
Dash of sea salt, or to taste	1 teaspoon dried thyme
2 carrots	1 teaspoon dried oregano
2 ribs celery	1 teaspoon white pepper
1 small onion, sliced	1 teaspoon garlic powder

Rub duck halves with hot sauce inside and out. Sprinkle with salt. In a baking pan that can be covered, place carrots, celery and onion IN THAT ORDER in the bottom of the pan in two piles. Place duck halves over the vegetables.

Thoroughly mix paprika, basil, thyme, oregano, white pepper and garlic powder. Coat duck skin with seasoning mix.

Cover pan and place in preheated 400-degree oven. Bake covered for at least 2 hours. Then, check for tenderness by twisting the duck leg. If the leg does not move easily, cover and return to the oven, checking every 20 minutes until leg does move easily. Total baking time can be anywhere from 2 hours to 4 hours, so be patient. When leg does turn easily, but meat is not quite falling from the bones, remove cover and return pan to the oven for another 15 minutes or until the skin browns.

Serve duck with wild rice and cold cranberry sauce on the side. A little wine? But, of course! Merlot and chardonnay are two excellent choices.

~ Lagniappé ~

For that extra special touch, pour off the duck fat and place drippings in blender with the roasted carrots, celery and onions. Blend until smooth, and add a little water to thin. This makes a wonderful sauce when poured over the duck just before serving.

Duck Étouffée

This is one of my favorite recipes for duck. Of course it has my own personal touch, and I think you'll find it great.

✦ Ⱨ ★

Yield: 4 servings as an entree, 8 as an appetizer

1 duck (5 to 5½ pounds),
   roasted according to recipe on page 94,
   reserve drippings
¼ cup butter or safflower oil
6 cups medium chopped white onions
3 cups diced green peppers
1½ cups diced celery
2 tablespoons chopped parsley
1 tablespoon dried sweet basil
1 tablespoon Louisiana hot sauce
   Dash of sea salt, or to taste
1 cup red wine (burgundy preferred)
2 tablespoons whole wheat pastry or unbleached flour

Remove and discard skin and bones from roasted duck. Shred meat and set aside.

Over low heat, melt butter until light brown or heat oil and add onions, peppers, celery, parsley, basil and hot sauce. Sauté until vegetables start to soften and begin to stick to the bottom of the pan, 15 to 20 minutes. Keep stirring, gently scraping the bottom of the pan to keep vegetables from burning.

Add ¼ cup water to deglaze pan, stirring thoroughly to loosen everything on the bottom. Continue to cook 2 to 3 minutes.

Stir in wine, flour, 1 cup water, duck meat and defatted duck drippings. Turn heat to low and simmer for 10 to 15 minutes. Check for salt content and add if needed. A sprinkle of cayenne will give this dish a little character!

Serve with wild rice and/or brown rice and garnish with green onion and parsley. A nice merlot is a great accompaniment to this dish.

Steak Dianne (for Two)

Cooking this dish may take a little practice,
but it is worth the trouble because it is one of the most wonderful
steak dishes ever created!

Yield: 2 servings

1	pound beef tenderloin, cut into eight 2-ounce pieces
1/4	cup Louisiana hot sauce, or to taste
1	teaspoon sea salt, or to taste
2	tablespoons unsalted butter
2	cups fresh sliced mushrooms
1	cup finely chopped green onions
2	tablespoons finely chopped parsley
2	cloves garlic, finely chopped
2	tablespoons Worcestershire sauce

Cover tenderloin pieces with hot sauce and salt. Set aside to marinate.

Place butter in a sauté pan. Set burner on low and heat butter until it begins to brown slightly.

Add mushrooms, green onions, parsley and garlic; sauté until vegetables are tender, 15 to 20 minutes. Move vegetables to side of pan and place medallions of beef in center.

Cook meat over medium-low heat 1½ minutes on one side. Turn and move vegetables back to the center of the pan, around the meat, and add Worcestershire sauce. Cook until desired doneness is achieved, another 1½ minutes for medium rare. If meat is to be cooked beyond medium rare, sauté the meat in a separate pan until almost done. Then finish cooking with the vegetables. This will prevent the vegetables from burning while the meat cooks to the extra doneness.

Although it is suggested that you serve this with natural brown rice, be sure to try pasta or your favorite potato side dish with it—they will complement this dish beautifully as well.

~ Lagniappe ~

You will find some recipes for Steak Dianne which call for flaming it
with cognac or brandy just prior to serving. I see no need to do this,
but you may want to try it to make a more dramatic presentation.

Sauces

What you conceive
You can achieve

North/South Cranberry Sauce

I operate a restaurant in cranberry country, so I've developed a recipe that combines the tangy northern fruit with a southern touch that's sure to please!

This sauce will hold in the refrigerator for months.

Yield: 10 to 12 servings

    1   pound whole cranberries, thawed if frozen
  1/2   cup brown sugar
  1/2   cup white sugar
  1/4   cup chopped pecans
  1/4   orange, chopped, rind and all
  1/4   lemon, chopped, rind and all
        Dash of cinnamon
    2   tablespoons dark rum or bourbon

In a stock pot over medium heat, bring cranberries, brown and white sugars, 1 cup water, pecans, orange, lemon and cinnamon to a boil. Stir this mixture as long as it is over heat to prevent sugars from burning and sticking. Boil for 2 minutes.

Remove from heat and allow to cool to room temperature, about 1 hour. Add liquor and again stir until well blended.

~ Lagniappé ~

*If you would like the sauce to be extra tart, reduce total sugar by 1/4 to 1/2 cup.
The 1 pound cranberry to 1 cup sugar to 1 cup water rule of thumb
is a good starting point for making your family's favorite cranberry sauce.*

Bayou Browned Garlic Butter Sauce

This sauce is for REAL garlic lovers ONLY!

The sauce will hold in the refrigerator for three to four days.

Yield: 1 1/4 cups

1   cup (2 sticks) unsalted butter
1   large bulb garlic, finely chopped
1/2 teaspoon sea salt, or to taste
1   tablespoon finely chopped fresh parsley

Melt butter on medium heat until slightly browned, stirring constantly to prevent burning.

Add garlic. Lower heat and sauté until garlic takes on the color of chopped roasted peanuts. Keep a close eye on pan when garlic starts to brown—a turn of the head and it will turn into charcoal.

Add salt and parsley, then sauté an additional 30 seconds.

Drizzle garlic sauce over your favorite seafood, poultry or steak— wonderful!

Chef Walter's Barbecue Sauce

This barbecue sauce is the base for several recipes you will find throughout Lagniappé.
*If you cannot buy my Bayou Cajun Barbecue Sauce in your area, you will find this
sauce will do a wonderful job in those recipes.*

Yield: 5 cups

2	cups tomato paste
1/3	cup molasses
1/4	cup dehydrated onions
3	tablespoons red wine vinegar
3	tablespoons sugar
1	tablespoon Worcestershire sauce
2	teaspoons liquid smoke
2	teaspoons dried oregano
1	teaspoon garlic powder
2	teaspoons cumin
1 1/3	teaspoons sea salt
1/2	teaspoon dry mustard
1/2	teaspoon cayenne
1/4	teaspoon crushed red pepper
1/4	teaspoon white pepper

In a stock pot, combine 2 cups water, tomato paste, molasses, dehydrated onions, vinegar, sugar, Worcestershire sauce, liquid smoke, oregano, garlic powder, cumin, sea salt, mustard, cayenne, red pepper and white pepper. Stir until ingredients are mixed together well and simmer for 1 hour. Continue to stir frequently throughout the cooking process to prevent sticking or burning. Store in jars in the refrigerator until ready to use.

Chicken Cream Sauce

While this sauce is wonderful on sautéed or roasted chicken,
try it too on veal or breaded sautéed fish.

Yield: 2¹/₂ cups

¹/₂ cup (1 stick) unsalted butter
¹/₂ cup whole wheat flour
 1   cup half-and-half
¹/₂ cup chicken stock (or drippings from roasting chicken)
 1   tablespoon chicken base
     Dash of Louisiana hot sauce

Over low heat, melt butter in a medium saucepan. Slowly add flour, while continually whisking, to make a light roux (page 51).

Add half-and-half and cook over low heat until mixture thickens, 6 to 7 minutes, continuing to stir to prevent sticking.

Add chicken stock, chicken base and hot sauce, and blend well. Simmer for about 5 minutes, stirring frequently.

Pour over roasted or sautéed chicken, and sprinkle with a garnish of chopped parsley. It's wonderful too with pasta, brown rice or your favorite potato dish.

Sauce Remoulade—French Style

*The origin of sauce remoulade can be found in France.
To the best of my knowledge, the following recipe comes closest
to the original French version. Designed to serve on shrimp,
it is also wonderful on cold meats, fish and salads.
Always serve it chilled.*

This sauce remoulade will hold in the refrigerator for weeks.

Yield: 1 1/2 cups

3   hard-boiled eggs
1   tablespoon white wine or tarragon vinegar
1   tablespoon prepared mustard
    Dash of sea salt, or to taste
    Dash of cayenne, or to taste
1/4   cup olive or safflower oil
    Juice from 1/2 lemon
1   clove fresh garlic, minced

Slice hard-boiled eggs in half. Remove yolks and place in a bowl, reserving egg whites. Mash yolks very fine and stir in wine, mustard, salt and cayenne.

Add oil in a slow steady stream, whisking continually to incorporate. Blend in lemon juice and garlic. Mix well and chill.

Crumble egg whites and sprinkle on sauce for garnish.

Remoulade Sauce—Louisiana Style

*This is the traditional sauce you'll find commonly served in New Orleans today.
It is mainly used over shrimp; however, with a little of your imagination,
I'll bet you can find other wonderful uses for it.*

This recipe will hold in the refrigerator for six months.

Yield: 4 cups

 2   cups mayonnaise
 2   cups Bayou Cajun Mustard
      or German-style mustard
 2   cloves garlic, finely chopped
12   green onions, finely chopped
1/2 cup finely chopped celery
 2   tablespoons Worcestershire sauce
 2   teaspoons lemon juice
1/2 teaspoon sugar
 2   tablespoons paprika
1/2 teaspoon Tabasco

Mix mayonnaise, mustard, garlic, onions, celery, Worcestershire sauce, lemon
juice, sugar, paprika and Tabasco together until well blended.

Chill at least 4 hours before serving to allow the flavors to "marry up."

Chef Walter's Remoulade Sauce

This is my version of Remoulade Sauce. I have used it for years in my restaurants with great acceptance. In fact, I bottle and sell it to the general public. You can see the difference in the remoulade sauces just by comparing recipes. They're all great, but I think mine is better!

Yield 2³/4 cups

1/2	stalk celery
6	green onions
6	sprigs parsley
1/4	cup red wine vinegar
1/4	cup safflower oil
1/4	cup dill relish
1/2	cup Bayou Cajun Mustard
	or German-style mustard
1/2	tablespoon hot sauce
1/2	tablespoon sea salt
1/2	tablespoon sifted paprika
1/2	teaspoon cayenne
	Juice of 1/4 lemon

Cut celery, onions and parsley into small pieces for grinding. Place in a food processor or meat grinder and grind to a medium consistency into a large bowl. Set aside.

In another bowl, mix vinegar, oil, dill relish, mustard, hot sauce, sea salt, paprika, cayenne and lemon juice, blending well.

Add this mixture to the ground mixture in the larger bowl and stir to combine. Refrigerate until well chilled, about 2 hours.

Serve over boiled shrimp, as a spread on bread, or with cold meat. Fantastic!

Master Creole Sauce

As you may have noticed, I have a few "Master" recipes, which are, as they imply, the base for several dishes that I make. Master Creole Sauce is no exception. I make Shrimp Creole at the Blue Bayou Inn, adding shrimp to the sauce and serving over a bed of rice. If your baked fish just doesn't sound exciting enough for dinner tonight, try it over rice topped with this zippy Creole sauce.

But don't just use it in the ways I've suggested—once you've worked up your own Creole sauce, take it another step and work up your very own culinary delights with it. The magic is truly in your hands.

This is a large recipe, but go ahead and make it up—what you don't use today freezes beautifully for a gourmet offering waiting for only a moment's notice. I recommend that you freeze the batch in portions, in plastic freezer bags, flattened so that it freezes quickly. The sauce will hold in the refrigerator for up to three days.

⚜ � ★

Yield: 6 cups

1 1/4	cups diced tomatoes	2	tablespoons safflower oil
1 1/4	cups crushed tomatoes	3/4	tablespoon thyme
	Juice of 1/4 lemon	1	teaspoon salt
1/2	cup white wine	1/2	teaspoon black or white pepper
1/2	green pepper, chopped medium	1/2	teaspoon crushed red pepper
2	stalks celery, chopped medium	1	bay leaf
1 1/2	cups medium chopped onion		Dash of cayenne
2 1/2	cloves garlic, chopped fine		

Combine tomatoes, lemon juice and wine in a large pot. Place pot over low heat and simmer while adding peppers, celery, onion, garlic, oil, thyme, salt, black or white pepper, red pepper, bay leaf and cayenne.

Continue to simmer 1 hour, until vegetables are tender and onions are translucent. Be sure to stir this mixture frequently to prevent scorching. Remove bay leaf. Serve as desired.

~ Lagniappe ~

This is Louisiana's answer to salsa, and can be used in any dish in place of salsa with excellent results.

Cajun Cocktail Sauce

Instead of tomato paste, tomato ketchup was originally called for in this recipe.
But Chef Walter has modified it because of ketchup's high sugar content.

Serve this sauce on the side accompanying shrimp or fish.
Shrimp can be marinated and served in this sauce if you wish.

Yield: 5 1/2 cups

2	cups chili sauce
2	cups tomato paste
1/4	cup Bayou Cajun Mustard
	or German-style mustard
1/2	cup horseradish
	Juice of 1/2 lemon
1	tablespoon Worcestershire sauce
1/4	cup chopped dill pickle relish
	Sea salt to taste
1/2	teaspoon Tabasco
	Dash of cayenne, optional

Combine chili sauce, tomato paste, mustard sauce, horseradish, lemon juice, Worcestershire, relish, salt, Tabasco and cayenne in bowl. Refrigerate until needed. Will hold under refrigeration for 1 month.

Bearnaise Sauce

*This is a classic sauce capable of turning
even ordinary everyday dishes
into gourmet treats.*

Yield: 1 cup

2   tablespoons tarragon vinegar
1/4 cup dry white wine
1/4 cup finely chopped shallots
2   tablespoons dried crushed tarragon leaves
2   tablespoons dried chervil
2   tablespoons fresh lemon juice
     Dash of salt
     Dash of pepper
3   egg yolks
2/3 cup butter
     Dash of cayenne, optional
2   tablespoons finely chopped fresh parsley

Combine vinegar, wine, shallots, tarragon leaves, chervil, lemon juice, salt and pepper in a medium saucepan. Boil over high heat, stirring constantly until mixture is reduced to 1/3 original volume. Strain and allow to cool about 10 minutes.

In the lower portion of a double boiler, heat water but do not allow it to boil. (Heating the water too hot will overcook the egg yolks in the mixture and the sauce will separate.) Place egg yolks, butter and cayenne in top of double boiler and whisk constantly until mixture is creamy and thick in texture and lemony in color.

Slowly add tarragon mixture and parsley, whisking constantly while adding. Allow to cool in the refrigerator until you are ready to serve. Reheat over double boiler before serving.

Lazy Man's Bearnaise Sauce:

*Use your favorite blender recipe for Hollandaise Sauce and add
1 tablespoon crushed tarragon leaves and 2 tablespoons white wine.*

Mornay Sauce

*This is a classic rich cheese sauce that is a delicious base
particularly wonderful with seafood and fish.*

This sauce should not be frozen. It will hold in the refrigerator for up to two days.

Yield: 2 cups

3	tablespoons butter
3	tablespoons whole wheat flour
1 1/2	cups scalded milk
	Dash of sea salt
2	ounces grated Swiss cheese
1/2	cup grated fresh Parmesan cheese
	Dash of Louisiana hot sauce

Over low heat, melt butter in a medium saucepan. Slowly whisk in flour, stirring continually, to make a light roux (page 51).

Continuing to cook over low heat, add milk and salt, stirring until smooth.

Add Swiss cheese and cook over low heat until well-blended. Remove from heat and stir Parmesan cheese and hot sauce into the mixture.

This is the delicious base for Crabmeat au Gratin (page 81).

Miscellaneous

Where ever you go—there you are!

Master Garlic Butter Supreme

*Master Garlic Butter Supreme is the basis for several other wonderful recipes,
but don't neglect to put it on the table for a delightful spread for bread or crackers
or baked potatoes!*

*Garlic Butter is the base ingredient for Shrimp De Jonghe (page 75),
Chicken De Jonghe (page 89) and Garlic Bread (page 114).*

*Master Garlic Butter Supreme is wonderful cut into medallions placed on top
of your favorite fish with thyme, oregano or sweet basil and baked at
350 to 375 degrees until the fish is done.*

Great on steak!

*It freezes beautifully, following the suggestions below,
or holds in the refrigerator for two to three weeks.*

Yield: 4 logs (1 cup each)

2	pounds unsalted butter
1	cup grated Parmesan cheese
1/2	cup garlic powder
1/2	cup finely chopped dried parsley
2	tablespoons paprika
2	tablespoons sea salt

Place butter in mixing bowl and allow to soften to room temperature, about 30 minutes.

Mix butter until whipped. Add each of the following, one at a time, mixing well after each addition: cheese, garlic powder, parsley, paprika and salt.

Divide garlic butter into 4 parts on sheets of wax paper and roll into logs 2 inches in diameter.

Refrigerate until firm, slicing off medallions of the garlic butter as needed (1/4-inch slice equals approximately 1 tablespoon). Hold in refrigerator for a few weeks, or double-wrap and retain in freezer for up to 6 months.

Bayou/Cajun Blended Flavors Barbecue Mixture

This is a unique blending of herbs and spices.
One day, some time ago, I was standing in my kitchen, looking at all the spices
and herbs I had on the shelves. A thought occurred (I know it's hard to believe!)—
what if I blend all these wonderful seasonings together. Well, I did, and a marvelous
blending of flavors occurred. By sprinkling this mixture over shrimp, fish or any of
your favorite seafood—you will create a taste that you've never experienced before.

Yield: 2 1/2 cups

2	tablespoons whole coriander	2	tablespoons whole fenugreek
2	tablespoons dried basil leaves	2	tablespoons whole fennel seed
1	tablespoon mace	2	tablespoons whole dried rosemary
2	tablespoons dry mustard	2	tablespoons seasoned salt
1	tablespoon ground allspice	1	teaspoon cayenne
1	tablespoon ground cloves	2	tablespoons salt
2	tablespoons ground marjoram	1	tablespoon ground black pepper
2	tablespoons whole mustard seed	2	tablespoons tarragon leaves
1	tablespoon turmeric	1	tablespoon chili powder
2	tablespoons whole celery seed	2	tablespoons dried leaf thyme
1	tablespoon crushed red pepper	2	tablespoons dried leaf oregano
2	tablespoons paprika	2	tablespoons dried chervil
2	tablespoons rubbed dried sage	1	tablespoon crushed bay leaves
1	tablespoon ground cumin seed		

In a large bowl, mix together all spices and herbs. Store in a cool dry place in a tightly sealed container.

Blackened Spice Mixture

*I recommend using Paul Prudhomme's excellent spice mixes if you want
a product you can take right off the shelf. He invented the process, and he is
"the man" where blackening is concerned, so don't be afraid to just go with that.
If you can't find it, or want to try making your own, here's my recipe.
Don't forget to add your own "magic."*

Yield: 3 tablespoons

1	tablespoon sweet paprika
1/2	teaspoon salt
1	teaspoon onion powder
1	teaspoon garlic powder
1	teaspoon red pepper (preferably cayenne)
3/4	teaspoon white pepper
3/4	teaspoon black pepper
1/2	teaspoon dried thyme leaves
1/2	teaspoon dried oregano leaves

Mix together all ingredients and transfer to a tightly sealed container. Store in a
cool, dry place.

Master Meat Marinade

*Master Meat Marinade is perfect for steaks headed for the charcoal grill or broiler.
It's wonderful for any kind of wild game. Try marinating beef tournedos in this for
six hours or overnight. The substitution of chicken base for beef base in the
recipe below converts this superb meat marinade into an equally wonderful
poultry and seafood marinade. If you have a sportsman in the house,
try this with wild game—it's superb!*

This marinade will hold in the refrigerator for up to one week.

Yield: 5 cups

1/2	tablespoon sea salt
1	teaspoon dried thyme
1	teaspoon black pepper
1	clove garlic, finely chopped
1	teaspoon oregano
1	tablespoon beef base
1	bay leaf
1/4	cup safflower oil
1	cup dry vermouth

Combine salt, thyme, black pepper, garlic, oregano, beef base, bay leaf, safflower
oil and 1 quart water in a large pot. Bring to a rapid boil over high heat. Remove from
heat and set aside to cool to room temperature, about 30 minutes. Remove bay leaf.

Add dry vermouth. If the vermouth is added to a hot mixture, it will lose its
power to marinate.

Garlic Bread

Garlic Bread is wonderful served with salad, soup or any entree.
Increase the amount of bread and garlic butter for the number of servings you desire.

Yield: 1 serving

1 slice **Master Garlic Butter Supreme, recipe on page 110**
1 slice bread, your favorite

Thaw garlic butter to room temperature. Spread bread with garlic butter. Place on a lightly oiled cookie sheet and bake in preheated 350-degree oven until browned, 5 to 7 minutes.

Croutons

*These croutons will make your delicious soups and salads memorable—
and use a leftover that too often goes to waste.
They're particularly well-suited for use on a Caesar salad.*

Yield: 12 cups

1   loaf day-old French or Italian bread
1   cup unsalted butter, or safflower or olive oil
1   teaspoon garlic salt
2   tablespoons Parmesan cheese, grated

Cut bread into rounds and lay on a cookie sheet. Melt butter and coat bread with butter, or oil. Preheat oven to 350-degrees and bake bread for 5 minutes or until golden brown. In a large bowl mix croutons with garlic salt and Parmesan cheese.

~ Lagniappé ~

Try using whole wheat bread—cut into cubes for a great unique taste!

Louisiana Oyster Dressing

This is a traditional Louisiana dressing, used there as a side dish—it's that good.
To stuff or not to stuff is entirely up to you and your family's taste; try it both ways!
Serve this delightful dressing as a side dish or stuff poultry or fish with it.

Dressing can be held in the refrigerator for up to three days.

⚜ ㅒ ★

Yield: 12 cups stuffing

1	quart shucked select oysters with water
8	cups cubed dried French or Italian bread
2	cups unsalted butter, divided
1/4	cup finely chopped parsley
1	stalk celery, chopped fine
12	green onions, chopped fine
5	cloves garlic, chopped fine
1	green pepper, chopped fine
2	tablespoons thyme
1	teaspoon white pepper
1	teaspoon cayenne
2	tablespoons sage
3	bay leaves
3	eggs, beaten
1/2	pound cubed pre-cooked turkey ham
	Sea salt to taste

Drain oysters and set aside. Soak bread in oyster water.

Over low heat, melt 1 cup of the butter in a large frying pan. Add parsley, celery, onion, garlic and green pepper. Sauté until vegetables are tender crisp, about 10 minutes. Set aside to cool for about 10 minutes.

Mix thyme, white pepper, cayenne, sage, bay leaves, eggs, turkey ham and salt into the soaked bread. Melt remaining 1 cup butter and stir into bread mixture. Stir in oysters and contents of the frying pan. Spread dressing in a 9x13-inch baking pan and bake in 350-degree oven until the dressing has a nice golden brown sheen on top, approximately 30 minutes. If dressing appears dry, add a little water. Remove bay leaves before serving.

Desserts

FLOYD SONNIER '89
MARDI GRAS GUMBO

Please *is like saying*
Thank you *in advance!*

Rice Fritters

✣ ♨ ★

1   cup cooked white or brown rice
1/2 cup unbleached flour or whole wheat pastry flour
1/4 tablespoon sugar or pure maple syrup
1/2 teaspoon double-acting baking powder
     Pinch of salt
3   eggs
     Vegetable oil for frying

Grind thoroughly cooled cooked rice in food processor and place into a large mixing bowl.

Combine flour, sugar, baking powder and salt in a separate bowl. Sift together over the rice.

Stir in eggs, one at a time, until absorbed by the mixture. Mixture should be the consistency of loose bread dough, i.e. it should clump easily. If mixture is too loose, add a little more flour.

Preheat 1 1/2 to 2 inches of oil to 350 degrees in a deep cast-iron saucepan, deep fat fryer or any heavy saucepan.

Drop batter, 1 tablespoon at a time, into the oil, cooking 5 to 6 fritters at a time. Fry until golden brown and crisp, about 3 minutes, turning after 1 1/2 minutes so that fritters brown evenly on both sides.

Remove from oil with a slotted spoon and transfer to paper towel to drain. Sprinkle with powdered sugar or top with maple syrup. Cut and serve warm with unsalted butter.

Bananas Foster

This is one of the all-time favorite desserts of New Orleans.

*In this recipe, do not use rum that is over 100 proof—
it can be very dangerous when flaming!*

Yield: 4 servings

1/3	cup unsalted butter
1/3	cup white granulated sugar
1/3	cup brown sugar
	Dash of ground cinnamon
2	ripe bananas, peeled, sliced in half lengthwise
3	tablespoons creme de banana liqueur
3	tablespoons dark rum
4	scoops vanilla ice cream

Melt butter in chafing dish with sugars and cinnamon. When ingredients start to bubble, add bananas.

Stir and flame mixture in chafing dish with banana liqueur. Turn bananas and flame with rum. It is essential that all alcohol is burned off to maximize flavor.

Scoop ice cream into 4 bowls. Place 1 banana over ice cream in each bowl. Serve immediately.

~ Lagniappé ~

Butter pecan or praline ice cream can be substituted for vanilla, to give this recipe a marvelous "down south" twist. Substitute praline liqueur for banana liqueur and serve over praline ice cream as suggested. I guarantee they'll jump out of their chair!

Chef Walter's Bayou Bread Pudding

There are two things great chefs of Louisiana argue over—
who has the best gumbo and, second, who has the best bread pudding.
Here's my version—I think it's the best you'll ever eat!

Yield: 12 servings

1/2	cup white granulated sugar
1/2	cup dark brown sugar
1/4	teaspoon cinnamon
3/4	cup white raisins
1/2	teaspoon nutmeg
1	cup (2 sticks) plus 2 teaspoons unsalted butter
4	loaves (12 inches each) day-old French or Italian bread
1	quart milk
3	eggs, whole or yolks only, beaten

Combine sugars, cinnamon, raisins, nutmeg and butter in a small pot. Heat over low heat, stirring constantly, 3 to 5 minutes. Set mixture aside to cool, 3 to 5 minutes.

Cube bread and place in a large mixing bowl. Pour milk over the bread.

Add sugar mixture to bread. Fold in eggs. Spread the entire mixture into a 9 x 13-inch baking pan with sides at least 2 inches high.

Cover pan with foil and bake in a preheated oven at 400 degrees for 1 hour. Remove foil and bake for an additional 5 to 10 minutes, until golden brown.

Remove from oven and allow to "rest" for a few minutes. Meanwhile, prepare Bourbon Street Whiskey Sauce (recipe on page 121). Dish out individual servings of bread pudding and top with sauce and whipped cream.

Bourbon Street Whiskey Sauce

*This sauce is designed to be the crowning glory on bread pudding,
but use your imagination. Try it on ice cream...vanilla...or go nuts and try it
on pecan or praline ice cream, cheesecake, coffeecake...is your mouth watering yet?*

Yield: 2¹/₂ cups

1/4 to 1/2	cup bourbon
1/2	cup white granulated sugar
1/2	cup brown sugar
1	cup (2 sticks) unsalted butter

Place bourbon and sugars in pot over low heat. Stir until sugars are melted. Add butter and melt. Heat an additional 2 minutes, stirring constantly. Remove from heat and serve hot. Sauce an be prepared ahead, cooled, refrigerated and reheated.

Bayou Dessert Crepes

Crepes for dessert are a fine French tradition. Use your imagination to create your own versions of this time-honored treat. The cooking of the crepe will take a little practice. Be patient with yourself and you will master it!

A whole egg may be substituted for the two egg yolks. The crepes will just be stiffer and drier.

Crepes will hold in the refrigerator for four to five days. Or fill the crepes and freeze them. To freeze without filling, stack crepes flat; when ready to serve, thaw completely so crepes won't tear as you try to pull them apart.

⚜ 卅 ★

Yield: 12 to 18 crepes

1 cup whole wheat pastry flour
2 tablespoons pure maple syrup or white granulated sugar
   Pinch of sea salt, optional
2 egg yolks
1 cup milk

1 teaspoon pure vanilla extract
4 tablespoons unsalted butter, melted or vegetable oil
1 teaspoon grated fresh orange peel, optional
4 tablespoons vegetable oil

Place flour, syrup, salt, egg yolks, milk, vanilla extract and melted butter into blender. Blend at high speed until well mixed, a few seconds. Turn blender off, scrape down sides and blend again for an additional 30 seconds. If orange peel is desired, stir in after blending.

Transfer batter to glass bowl. Let batter rest at room temperature for at least 2 hours before using.

To cook, use only steel or stainless steel 8-inch crepe pan or skillet. Heat over high heat until a drop of water flicked into pan sputters and evaporates instantly. Remove pan from heat, but keep burner on. Dip corner of a paper or cloth towel in vegetable oil and coat pan with a thin layer of oil.

Whisk batter lightly just before ladling into pan. Use a small ladle to pour 1/4 cup batter into the pan, circling until the entire surface is covered. Pour excess batter back into the bowl.

Return pan to heat and cook until crepe edge begins to brown. Turn by pulling with the edge of butter knife or spatula. Cook second side for about 1 minute, then slide onto a plate and cool about 10 minutes. Finished crepe should be very thin.

Once cool, crepes can be wrapped and refrigerated or frozen. Return crepes to room temperature before separating.

Crepes Suzette

✦ 끼 ★

1/3 cup orange juice
1/4 cup unsalted butter
 2 tablespoons sugar
1/4 teaspoon grated fresh orange peel

Over low heat stir juice, butter, sugar and orange peel until mixture is warm and sugar is dissolved. Serve over crepes.

~ Lagniappé ~

1. *Fill with praline ice cream, top with Bourbon Street Whiskey Sauce (recipe on page 121) and whipped cream.*

2. *For Crepes Fitzgerald, fill with cream cheese mixture.*

3. *For Crepes McFarland, pour hot cranberry sauce (North/South Cranberry Sauce on page 98) over crepes and top with whipped cream.*

4. *Fill with your favorite fruit mixture.*

Mocha Mousse

This dessert is an original of mine.
I developed it for a customer who was an avid coffee lover.
You'll find that it is the perfect crowning touch to any great meal.
It has a pleasant taste and a texture light as a feather!

Mocha Mousse can be portioned out in individual servings,
covered with food wrap and refrigerated for up to five days.

Yield: 8 servings

2   tablespoons freeze-dried coffee
2   tablespoons coffee-flavored brandy, or Kahlua or Tia Maria
1/2   cup confectioners' sugar
1   teaspoon vanilla
2   cups whipping cream

Place coffee, coffee-flavored brandy, sugar and vanilla into a medium-sized bowl. Set mixer at low speed and mix until all ingredients are thoroughly blended.

Add whipping cream and set speed to high. Mix until cream turns to mousse texture, or forms soft peaks.

Scoop into 1 cup servings. Top with additional whipped cream, sprinkle with freeze-dried coffee and serve.

Amaretto Almond Cream Supreme

This is a wonderful dessert to prepare ahead.
Just wrap pie tightly and freeze until ready to serve.
It's a good idea to cut into sections before freezing
if you would like access to individual portions.

✦ Ⱨ ★

Yield: 12 servings

1   can (14 ounces) condensed milk
1/2 cup amaretto liqueur
2   tablespoons chocolate syrup
1   pint whipping cream plus additional for garnish
1   graham cracker pie shell (9 inches)
1   bag (1 ounce) sliced almonds

Blend together condensed milk, amaretto and chocolate syrup.

Pour whipping cream into a separate mixing bowl and beat until soft peaks form. Fold amaretto mixture into whipping cream and pour into pie shell. Garnish with almonds, slice into individual portions and freeze until firm.

When ready to serve, top portions with whipped cream. Whipping cream in a refrigerated aerosol can is most convenient for garnish at serving time.

Chocolate Pecan Praline Pie or Tart

This is Rita's dessert, and she recommends the Keebler brand of chocolate graham cracker pie shell for best results.

When my son Matt hears the beaters,
he's in the kitchen to lick the bowl before it's even done!

Yield: 15 servings

1	can (14 ounces) sweetened condensed milk
1/2	cup praline liqueur
2	tablespoons chocolate syrup
1	pint whipping cream plus additional for garnish
15	pecan halves
1	chocolate graham cracker pie shell (9 inches) or 15 chocolate graham cracker tart shells

Blend together condensed milk, praline liqueur and chocolate syrup. Beat whipping cream in a small bowl until soft peaks form. Fold praline mixture into whipping cream and pour into pie shell or tart shells. Garnish with pecans and freeze until firm.

Slice into individual portions and top with whipped cream at serving time. Whipping cream in refrigerated aerosol can is most convenient for garnish.

Pumpkin Slices

This is one of Rita's favorite cheesecake recipes.
Make a big batch and freeze some for later....

This dessert will hold in the refrigerator for five days and freezes very well too.

Yield: 12 servings

1	envelope (1/4 ounce) unflavored gelatin
1/4	cup cold water
2	cups cooked pumpkin or 1 can (16 ounces)
3	eggs, separated
3/4	cup sugar, divided
1/2	cup milk
1/2	teaspoon salt
1	teaspoon cinnamon

Crust:

2	cups graham cracker crumbs
1/3	cup sugar
1/2	cup butter or margarine

Cream Cheese Layer:

2	eggs
3/4	cup sugar
1	package (8 ounces) cream cheese (do not use whipped cream cheese)

Dissolve gelatin in cold water. Over low heat, combine pumpkin, egg yolks, 1/2 cup of the sugar, milk, salt and cinnamon. Heat and stir constantly until mixture thickens, about 10 minutes. Remove from heat and add gelatin mixture. Cool completely, in refrigerator, about 20 minutes.

Meanwhile, prepare crust. Mix graham crackers, sugar and butter. Press into a 9x13-inch pan.

Make cream cheese layer by mixing eggs, sugar and cream cheese together. Pour over crust and bake for 20 minutes at 350 degrees. Set aside to cool.

Beat egg whites and remaining 1/4 cup sugar until stiff. Fold into cooled pumpkin mixture.

Pour pumpkin mixture over cooled cream cheese layer and refrigerate until set. To serve, top with fresh whipped cream and chopped pecans.

Rita's Cheesecake

This recipe has been used and developed by my wife Rita.
You will find it both easy and wonderful—like she is!

This cheesecake freezes very nicely,
or you can hold it in the refrigerator for up to one week.

Yield: 12 servings

2 1/2	cups graham crackers crumbs
1/3	cup sugar
2/3	cup butter, melted
1	package (1 pound) marshmallows
3/4	cup milk
2	packages (8 ounces each) cream cheese
1	cup whipping cream

Blend crumbs, sugar and melted butter together. Remove 3/4 cup of mixture and set aside for topping. Press remaining mixture into the bottom of a 9x13-inch pan.

Place marshmallows and milk in the top of a double boiler over hot water and heat until melted. Turn mixture into mixing bowl and add cream cheese.

Beat until cheese mixture is smooth and has the consistency of custard, about 5 minutes. Cool about 10 minutes at room temperature.

In a separate bowl, beat whipping cream until soft peaks form. Fold whipped cream into cheese mixture and pour into pan over graham cracker crust. Top with remaining crumbs. Refrigerate 4 to 7 hours.

Slice and serve topped with fresh strawberries, pecan or cranberry sauce and a dab of whipped cream.

Index

✦ ⚜ ★

About the Artist...

Lagniappé was illustrated by Louisiana artist Floyd Sonnier, whose drawings have adorned the walls, menus and signs of Walt Mazur's restaurants since he discovered him in the 1970's. Now they provide authentic Louisiana charm to Walt's cookbook. He wanted you to know a little more about this business associate who quickly became a very dear friend. I had the pleasure of interviewing him for this piece in 1992 and only hope I was able to convey in some small way the warmth and charm of this delightful man.

"Floyd Sonnier is just a beautiful guy," says Chef Walter, "and beautiful is as beautiful does in his case." He explained that he encountered Sonnier's work while operating his Cajun House in Chicago. He fell in love with the drawings from Louisiana that artistically dramatized the bayou feeling he was creating with his food and atmosphere.

Deciding he could enhance his ambiance with this wonderful art, he contacted Floyd and ordered prints to display and contracted with him to design menu and sign adornments for his restaurant. He expanded on the line when he moved north to open Blue Bayou Inn, covering the walls with Floyd's unique portrayals of bayou life.

"Floyd would be my artist in residence if he lived here, but it's just too cold for him," Walt laughs. "We use his stuff on everything from our logo on cards and letterheads, to menu decoration and now illustrating our cookbook. We've surrounded ourselves and our customers with his artwork, hanging on every wall of the restaurant."

Like the food Chef Walter brings to his customers in his restaurant, cooking school and now his cookbook, Floyd Sonnier's artwork is "the real thing." It doesn't just look like bayou country, it IS bayou country.

Born and raised in the heart of Louisiana's bayous, Floyd Sonnier has been drawing since he was three years old. And everything he did from day one depicted the home he loves.

Even when he had to pursue other endeavors to make a living, he continued to draw Louisiana bayou scenes, richly endowed with authentic cultural and historic detail. Finally in the mid-1970's, he took the big step of quitting his full-time job to devote all of his time and attention to his artwork.

Floyd Sonnier was born into the Acadian culture, which brought rich traditions with them when they migrated to Louisiana from Nova Scotia 230 years ago. He calls his art company "Beau Cajun Art," and his motto is printed as a subtitle wherever the name of the company appears: "Dedicated to the preservation of Acadian Culture."

His heritage is inextricably interwoven with his artwork, endowing each piece with a depth and rich history absent in so much of today's art. Once you've seen any of Sonnier's work, you will have no trouble identifying more when you see it.

His style is distinctive and haunts the viewer with a gripping image of another time and place. He takes you to his beloved bayou country with compelling images of people and places alien to our 1990's world, but inviting because of their down-home warmth.

They invade your imagination with nostalgia for the charm of simpler times and simpler lives that prevailed in rural America. And they hint that there may be a few places you can still go for a taste or glimpse of those simpler times.

In that respect, Sonnier's artwork issuing from the far Northwoods of Wisconsin is unexpectedly appropriate. Far removed from urban sprawl, the Northwoods is as close to its rustic roots as it is to the modern world. A kind of crossroads.

On the main drag you see civilization prevail, but a mile out of town, on a sideroad winding to one of thousands of lakes, it's easy to perceive the less-complicated past. This respite from the modern world, located a few hours north of several urban centers, is the basis for this area's magnetism to vacationers.

And as his artwork centers around old-fashioned charm, Floyd's life is based on old-fashioned ideals. He credits God for his talent, and expresses a need to take that gift very seriously and use it to share the beauty in his world with the rest of us. For that WE can thank God, for his work really is a special treat to behold. It's a journey of the eye and the mind to another time and place.

True to his down-home roots, Floyd's attitude toward the business of his art is secondary to his desire to truly live a full life through it. He is fiercely proud of the culture he portrays, and is bent on preserving his heritage through his drawings.

Chef Walter says Floyd Sonnier is a beautiful guy. And so he is. When you talk to Floyd, you never stay a business contact for long. His musical Cajun drawl is so comforting to listen to, and accompanied by such warmth that he feels like a friend two minutes into your first conversation. And he doesn't disappoint later.

He kept inviting Chef Walter to visit after that first order. Finally his telephone friend managed a trip south. Floyd reports their first meeting this way:

"I had no idea what he looked like. He didn't send me a picture, but we talked on the phone so often I really wanted to meet the guy. I was in a show at Baton Rouge, and it was going pretty slow, so I was watching the door."

"About a half hour into the show, in walks this huge guy wearing a suit and carrying a briefcase. I took one look at this guy—who was now heading straight toward me. I thought, 'this has GOT to be the IRS, nobody else would look like that.' Plus he looked real mean. He came right up to my display, then he stretched out that big hand across the table and said 'Hi, I'm Walt Mazur.'

"I invited him to my home the next day for breakfast, and he's been coming down to visit every year since, and spends a few days with us. He's no stranger in Louisiana, you know."

Chef Walter, in turn, got after Floyd to venture north to see his Blue Bayou Inn. Finally in 1990, a friend with a small plane flew Sonnier and his wife to visit—in July.

"Have you ever been up in a small plane there?" he asks, in the midst of telling about his trip. "We got there and we just couldn't believe all the lakes and rivers. We had trouble spotting that little airstrip at first, but we found it. What a beautiful area from the air."

Floyd enjoyed his venture to the Northwoods, but he's a Louisiana boy to stay. He explains that when it gets down to 30 degrees there in winter, that's plenty cold for him. A year in Germany in his youth further convinced him that he was in Louisiana to stay once he got home.

If you enjoy Floyd's wonderful artwork and would like to obtain his catalog and price list, you can get a free brochure on all available limited edition prints and his calendars at the Beau Cajun Art Gallery, PO Box 397, Scott, Louisiana 70583, 318-237-7104.

The Last Word

✦ 出 ★

He was 13 years my senior. I was 17.

How did we meet? Of course, it was through the restaurant industry. I was planning a banquet when I let my fingers do the walking through the yellow pages and found an interesting place on Lake Shore Drive in Chicago called the Lake Tower Inn. Who do you think was the manager?

The one and only Walter G. Mazurkiewicz! Two weeks later a cab arrived to pick me up for our first date. That evening was followed with roses! He performed those "magical niceties" that caused a young girl to become very interested. Wally was very spontaneous and even then he lived for the moment!

The spontaneity continued. We were married and honeymooned in Tahiti! Four months later he came home and said, "Let's go for a ride. I'm going to show you our new restaurant!"

We had about $500 in the bank, I was pregnant with our daughter Penny and I informed him that he was crazy!

It was 1974, and we named the restaurant the Cajun House on Diversey. After five years of hard work we had a successful business, but now Wally needed a "new" challenge. I was given the choice between going North or South. I decided I wanted to go "as far North as the South is ever gonna get!"

We bought a restaurant and home in Manitowish Waters and settled there. The name Blue Bayou Inn was carefully chosen to tell customers what we have to offer. "Blue" for the sky (you can see a lot of it out the bank of glass windows in the dining room). "Bayou" for the water which the dining room overlooks on two sides. And Walt felt that "Inn" conveyed a feeling of relaxation in an elegant atmosphere—perfect for our guests to dine in and enjoy.

It was 1980. By now I was pregnant with our son Joe, hoping this isn't a trend in our lives—new restaurant and new baby every five years?

Anyway, Wally wanted a challenge and he got one! But once Walt listened to the inner self and let his spontaneity take over, our Blue Bayou became successful. If for no other reason because Walt was running things the way he wanted.

His craziness surfaced to include the "Angler's Special," "Dine With Walter," and "The Louisiana School of Cooking in Wisconsin."

And then there was the Limo—he purchased it and gave it to me for our wedding anniversary. (All I wanted to know was "Where's the payment book?") I guess all of these ideas and more were that "crunch" that he gave and will continue to give through the publishing of his book.

Well, five years passed, and lo and behold, Rita's pregnant with number two son Matthew and guess what? This time we're NOT buying a restaurant!

The Blue Bayou now involved the entire family, including my mom Rita and my dad Joe. Everyone was assigned their tasks to perform. My dad has died, but Mom is still here to help. Some of you may have enjoyed one of her "special occasion" cakes.

The Northwoods changed our family and our lifestyle. Wally ate healthier, he thought healthier and he developed a more positive outlook. But most of all, his spiritual belief and closeness to God became more apparent.

I can't explain how someone who loved us and life so very much became ill so quickly and died from cancer on March 18th of 1994. We were married just 30 days short of our 20th anniversary. I wish all of you could have gotten by that "gruff," "hard" exterior and have known the soft warm fuzzy interior of the dynamic man I knew and loved.

Before I close I need to say "thank you" to Barb who started this project with Walt over six years ago and continued "prodding" us to completion.

To Penny, my daughter and friend who worked very hard to accomplish this. Your dad is very proud and so am I.

To my boys Joe and Matt, know that Mom is always here for you and your dad is with us in spirit.

To my mom for always supporting and loving me.

To Tom, Matt, Pam, Howie and staff, who helped proof recipes and have been my support to keep the Bayou operating.

To all of my family and friends and acquaintances who have helped me in one way or another. I love you all.

I will close with a poem and say "thank you" Wally for those footprints.

—Rita Mazur

Some people

come into our lives

and quickly go....

Some stay for awhile

and leave footprints

on our hearts

And we are never

ever the same

Come on in...

and try these recipes recreated by our fine chefs at the Blue Bayou Inn. Make your reservations today for an experience in dining excitement...call 715-543-2537. The Blue Bayou Inn in beautiful Manitowish Waters is easy to find; just head north or south on Highway 51 and meet at the "4-star restaurant." The Blue Bayou is just north of Manitowish Waters Bridge. Open seasonally, late April through October.

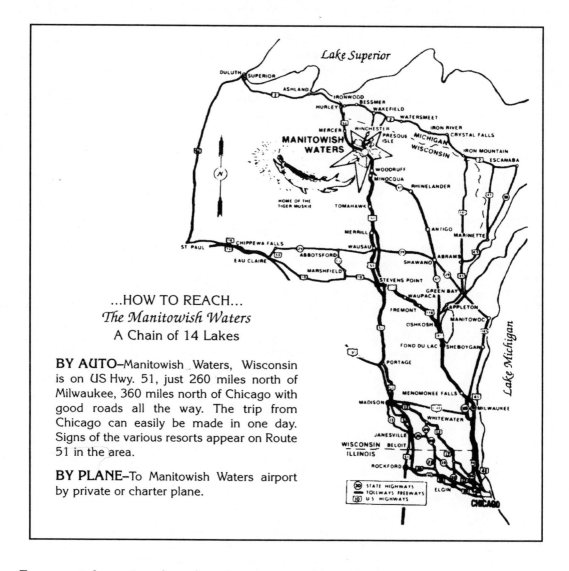

...HOW TO REACH...
The Manitowish Waters
A Chain of 14 Lakes

BY AUTO–Manitowish Waters, Wisconsin is on US Hwy. 51, just 260 miles north of Milwaukee, 360 miles north of Chicago with good roads all the way. The trip from Chicago can easily be made in one day. Signs of the various resorts appear on Route 51 in the area.

BY PLANE–To Manitowish Waters airport by private or charter plane.

For more information about *Lagniappé* or to order our special cajun sauces, write to:

Blue Bayou Inn
Hwy 51 at the Spider Lake Bridge
PO Box 115
Manitowish Waters, WI 54545

"The exterior polar bear and the interior teddy bear! We loved Walt..."

"The good times..."

"Wally the Clown—the days we went to hospitals to entertain children—the unselfish ways of Wally my friend..."

"I remember all the meals he cooked at my house and helping me out on holidays—and all the meals we had at the restaurants..."

"Working with Walt to write an article about the Blue Bayou for Who's Who in the Northwoods... working with him at the reception for the new Marshfield Clinic and at the Holiday Homestead for the March of Dimes Chef's Auction...The only guy I ever spilled wine on serving at the Guides' Inn...I remember last seeing him at the WRA Christmas party at Polecat in December of '93. I'll miss him..."

"I will always remember..."

"Four years ago, stopping at the Blue Bayou. When word got to the kitchen that some "mad islanders" were there, we were welcomed like old friends and treated like kings. And the food! Like nothing I've ever experienced before or since. I will never forget...Thanks Walt!"

"How helpful and generous Walt was with his time and advice to a newcomer..."

"Walt was the cornerstone of our club (St. Anthony's Men's Club).... always willing to do for others...we will miss him..."